Anth
Dr. Sher

The Runaway Bride of Christ

Overcoming Church Hurt

Contributing Authors:
Ashley Thompson
Dr. Ebony Michelle Collins
Leah Clement
Lillie B. Randle

Copyright © 2024 Dr. Sherley Lefevre, Ph.D.

All rights reserved. No part of this book may be reproduced, stored, or transmitted by any means—whether auditory, graphic, mechanical, or electronic—without written permission of both publisher and author, except in the case of brief excerpts used in critical articles and reviews. Unauthorized reproduction of any part of this work is illegal and is punishable by law.

Contents

Introduction: The Runaway Bride by Dr. Sherley Lefevre v

PART I
TEACHING CHAPTERS

The Bride of Christ by Dr. Sherley Lefevre 1
Leading God's People According to the Bible by Dr. Sherley Lefevre 13
Narcissism within the Church Walls by Dr. Sherley Lefevre 27
Religious Spirits vs. The Holy Spirit by Ashley Thompson 41

PART II
TESTIMONY CHAPTERS

From the Depths of Betrayal to the Heights of Triumph 59
Heavenly First Love by Ashley Thompson 71
From the Parking Lot to the Pulpit by Dr. Ebony Michelle Collins 97
Burnt Alive 109
All Eyes Are On Us 119
Poetry Reflections 129

PART III
SCRIPTURES & PRAYERS

Introduction: The Runaway Bride

By Dr. Sherley Lefevre

In the shadows of stained-glass windows, choir robes, and beautiful pews lies a narrative often whispered but seldom acknowledged: the peril of church hurt. It's a story etched in the tears of the wounded, a symphony of shattered trust and broken spirits that reverberates through the hallowed halls of congregations worldwide. This is not a book about ancient history or distant lands; it is a raw and potent reality that permeates the very fabric of our communities today.

Welcome to a journey that delves into the depths of human frailty and the resilience of the soul. In these pages, you will encounter stories of betrayal and redemption, of faith tested in the crucible of pain, and of triumph born from the ashes of despair. This is not merely a collection of anecdotes. It is a testament to the power of God's grace to heal even the deepest wounds and to transform lives shattered by church hurt into beacons of hope and resilience.

As you embark on this exploration, prepare to confront uncomfortable truths and challenge preconceived notions. Church hurt is not a topic for

Dr. Sherley Lefevre, Ph.D.

the faint of heart; it is a sobering reminder of the imperfections that lurk within the walls of even the holiest sanctuaries. Yet, it is also a rallying cry for change, a call to action to reclaim the purity of our faith communities and to create spaces of genuine love and acceptance.

Through the lens of personal experiences and biblical wisdom, we will navigate the treacherous waters of betrayal, abuse, and exclusion that plague so many. But fear not, for this is also a journey of hope; a journey that leads from the depths of despair to the heights of triumph, where wounds are healed and scars become badges of honor.

So, dear reader, fasten your seatbelt and prepare to embark on a journey of emotions and revelations. This is not just a book; it is a lifeline for those drowning in the tumultuous seas of church hurt and a guiding light pointing to the shores of healing and redemption. Welcome to "The Runaway Bride of Christ: Overcoming Church Hurt," a journey that will challenge, inspire, and ultimately transform you.

If you have experienced any church hurt throughout your Christian journey, my prayer is that this book will serve as a tool to help you heal and find purpose in your pain. May this book bring revelation and empowerment to you as you confront and overcome church hurt as the Bride of Christ.

About Visionary Dr. Sherley Lefevre

Dr. Sherley Lefevre, a native of Brooklyn, New York, and of Haitian descent, has walked a path marked by trials and triumphs. From overcoming the trauma of molestation to surviving domestic violence, Dr. Sherley has faced significant hardships throughout her life. Yet, her unwavering love for God and passion for spreading the love of Jesus Christ have remained steadfast.

A dedicated Nurse by profession, Dr. Sherley holds both a bachelor's and master's degree in nursing and is currently pursuing her doctorate in Nursing. Her academic pursuits extend beyond healthcare; she is also well-versed in theology, having earned a master's in divinity (MDiv) and a Ph.D.

in Practical Ministry. In recognition of her dedication to faith and service, Dr. Sherley was honored in 2023 with two prestigious honorary doctorates: a Doctorate in Christian Humanities from the School of the Great Commission and a Doctor of Divinity from the United Kingdom Abyssinia Christ-Centered Theological Seminary.

Dr. Sherley is the esteemed host of the podcast and international radio show, "A Word with Dr. Sherley," which airs on major platforms and Envisioned Broadcasting Radio station. As a Certified Christian Counselor, she specializes in grief, trauma, women's issues, and relationships. Her expertise and compassion have made her a sought-after international speaker and bestselling author, with five books to her name.

As the visionary founder of Beauty for Ashes Global, a non-profit, faith-based organization, Dr. Sherley is deeply committed to women's empowerment and spiritual growth. The organization provides Christian Bible teaching and resources through various channels, including books, sermons, intercessory prayers, evangelical missions, and community outreach. With a dual mission to serve both locally and globally, Beauty for Ashes Global offers strength and hope to those in despair, facilitating spiritual growth through virtual meetings, daily inspirational posts on social media, and global evangelistic outreach events.

Dr. Sherley's calling to counsel, inspire, and empower others on their spiritual journeys is evident in her work. Her newest venture, Grace Divine Enterprises, further expands her impact by offering publishing services to aspiring and seasoned authors, as well as coaching services to support Christian entrepreneurs and leaders. Additionally, her life coaching services extend to those navigating hurt and trauma, helping them find effective paths to healing and forward momentum. Empowered by her own experiences, Dr. Sherley Lefevre continues to be a beacon of resilience, faith, and empowerment, dedicated to uplifting others and guiding them on their spiritual journeys. To learn more about Dr. Sherley please visit http://www.drsherleyphd.com

Other Works by Dr. Sherley Lefevre

- *His Beauty for My Ashes Anthology*
- *The Purge: Breaking Chains, Renewing Legacies Anthology*
- *The Purge Daily Devotional*
- *Queen Esther's Royal Code Anthology (Contributor)*

PART I
Teaching Chapters

The Bride of Christ

By Dr. Sherley Lefevre

(All scriptures were taken from the New International Version of the Bible)

In the area of Christian theology, the metaphor of the Church as the "Bride of Christ" is embedded with profound significance. This chapter delves into the depth of this imagery, exploring what it means for us as individuals and as a collective body of believers to embody this identity. Through unity, love, and devotion, we find not only our purpose but also our strength. As we reflect on the profound imagery of the Bride of Christ, may we be inspired to embody unity, love, devotion, and commitment in our journey of faith. May we strive to be a faithful and radiant Bride, reflecting the love and glory of our Bridegroom, Jesus Christ, to the world around us.

The Church as the Bride of Christ: An Exploration

The metaphor of the Church as the Bride of Christ is deeply rooted in Christian theology and has profound implications for understanding the relationship between Christ and His Church. This metaphorical framework draws upon biblical imagery, particularly from the New Testament, to describe the intimate and covenantal bond between Jesus Christ and the community of believers known as the Church. In this chapter, we will explore the theological significance, biblical foundations, historical interpretations, and practical implications of the Church as the Bride of Christ.

Theological Significance

At the heart of the metaphor lies the theological concept of covenantal love and union. The relationship between Christ and the Church is portrayed not merely as a contractual or legalistic bond but as a deeply personal and sacrificial union. This imagery emphasizes the unconditional love of Christ for His people, akin to the self-sacrificial love of a husband for his bride, as described in Ephesians 5:25-27: "Husbands, love your wives, just as Christ loved the church and gave himself up for her to make her holy, cleansing her by the washing with water through the word, and to present her to himself as a radiant church, without stain or wrinkle or any other blemish, but holy and blameless."

The Bride of Christ metaphor underscores the Church's identity as the beloved of God, chosen and cherished by Him. It highlights the purity and sanctity of the Church, which Christ sanctifies and prepares for Himself. This theological understanding encourages believers to perceive themselves not only as members of a religious institution but as participants in a divine romance, where God's love for His people is celebrated in the context of a loving and committed relationship.

Biblical Foundations

The imagery of the Church as the Bride of Christ finds its roots in various passages throughout the New Testament. One of the most prominent is found in the Book of Revelation, where the marriage supper of the Lamb is described as a symbol of the ultimate union between Christ and His Church. Revelation 19:7-9 portrays this vividly: "Let us rejoice and be glad and give him glory! For the wedding of the Lamb has come, and his bride has made herself ready. Fine linen, bright and clean, was given to her to wear. (Fine linen stands for the righteous acts of God's holy people.) Then the angel said to me, 'Write this: Blessed are those who are invited to the wedding supper of the Lamb!' And he added, 'These are the true words of God.'"

Furthermore, the metaphor is echoed in the teachings of Jesus Himself, particularly in His parables and teachings about the Kingdom of God. In Matthew 22:2-14, Jesus tells the parable of the wedding banquet, illustrating God's invitation for all people to participate in the joyous celebration of His Kingdom.

Practical Implications

The metaphor of the Church as the Bride of Christ has practical implications for Christian faith and practice. It calls believers to embody the virtues of love, fidelity, and purity in their relationships with God and one another. It challenges the Church to reflect the sacrificial love of Christ in its mission and ministry, serving as a beacon of hope and reconciliation in a broken world.

Moreover, the metaphor invites believers to cultivate a deep sense of identity and belonging within the Church as the beloved community of God. It encourages spiritual growth and discipleship as believers strive to live out their faith in alignment with God's purposes and values.

Overall, the metaphor of the Church as the Bride of Christ is a rich and multifaceted theological concept that illuminates the profound mystery of God's love for His people. Rooted in biblical imagery, affirmed throughout Christian history, and relevant to contemporary faith, this metaphor invites believers into a deeper understanding of their identity, purpose, and relationship with God through Jesus Christ. It calls the Church to embody the transformative power of divine love and to bear witness to God's kingdom in anticipation of the ultimate wedding feast of the Lamb.

Love as the Foundation

At the heart of the metaphor lies the concept of love. Just as a bride and groom are bound together by love so, too, are we bound to Christ by His unconditional love for us. This love serves as the foundation upon which our faith is built and the guiding principle for how we interact with one another. Let us emulate Christ's love in our words, actions, and attitudes, fostering an environment of acceptance, compassion, and grace.

The Gospel of John emphasizes the centrality of love in the relationship between Christ and His Church in John 15:12-13: "My command is this: Love each other as I have loved you. Greater love has no one than this: to lay down one's life for one's friends."

Unity in Diversity

Just as a bride is adorned with various jewels, the Church is enriched by the diversity of its members. Each individual brings a unique perspective, gift, and story to the faith community. Rather than allowing differences to divide us, let us celebrate the richness of our diversity and embrace unity in Christ.

The Apostle Paul beautifully illustrates this unity amidst diversity in 1 Corinthians 12:12-14: "Just as a body, though one, has many parts, but all its many parts form one body, so it is with Christ. For we were all baptized by one Spirit so as to form one body—whether Jews or Gentiles, slave or free—and we were all given the one Spirit to drink. Even so the body is not made up of one part but of many."

Devotion and Commitment

The image of a bride also signifies devotion and commitment. As the Bride of Christ, we are called to wholeheartedly devote ourselves to Him, prioritizing our relationship with Him above all else. This devotion is not passive but requires active participation in the life of the Church, serving one another with humility, generosity, and sacrificial love.

The Apostle Peter encourages believers to live in devotion to Christ and one another in 1 Peter 4:8-10: "Above all, love each other deeply, because love covers over a multitude of sins. Offer hospitality to one another without grumbling. Each of you should use whatever gift you have received to serve others, as faithful stewards of God's grace in its various forms."

Restoration and Redemption

Just as a bridegroom cherishes his bride, Christ lovingly pursues His Church, seeking her restoration and redemption. Despite our flaws and failures, His grace abounds, offering forgiveness, healing, and transformation. This aspect of the metaphor highlights the profound depth of Christ's love and His relentless pursuit of reconciliation with His people.

Let us embrace this redemptive journey, allowing Christ to renew and refine us, individually and collectively, into the radiant Bride He envisions. The redemptive journey as the Bride of Christ involves both personal and communal aspects. Individually, believers are called to repentance and faith, turning away from sin and embracing Christ's forgiveness and healing. Collectively, the Church as a whole undergoes a continual process of renewal and refinement, guided by the Holy Spirit to grow in unity and maturity.

Renewal and Refinement

Christ desires His Church to reflect His glory and character to the world. This requires ongoing renewal and refinement, where believers cooperate with the Holy Spirit in sanctification; the process of becoming holy and set apart for God's purposes. Philippians 1:6 assures us of God's faithfulness in this transformative work: "Being confident of this, that he who began a good work in you will carry it on to completion until the day of Christ Jesus."

Dr. Sherley Lefevre, Ph.D.

Christ's Pursuit of His Church

The pursuit of the bridegroom for his bride in traditional marriage customs symbolizes dedication and commitment. Similarly, Christ's pursuit of His Church is marked by His unfailing love and desire for intimate communion with His people. The prophet Hosea vividly portrays this divine pursuit in Hosea 2:14-16, where God speaks of wooing His unfaithful people back to Himself with tenderness and compassion.

A Love Beyond Measure

Just as a devoted bridegroom seeks his beloved with unwavering determination, Christ's pursuit of His Church transcends human understanding. His love is not merely an abstract concept, but a relentless pursuit of hearts turned astray. In Hosea's touching depiction, God promises to draw His people into the wilderness, where He will speak tenderly to their hearts, drawing them back into a covenant of love and fidelity.

The narrative of Hosea reflects the enduring theme of reconciliation and restoration within the Church. Despite human frailty and waywardness, Christ continues to extend His hand, beckoning His beloved to return to Him. This divine pursuit serves as a testament to the unchanging nature of God's love; a love that surpasses all failures and transgressions, seeking to heal and restore.

Embracing the Call to Fidelity

In the wake of discord and disarray, the Church is called to emulate the fidelity depicted in the divine pursuit of Hosea. Just as Christ pursues His Bride with unwavering devotion, the Church must reaffirm its commitment to the gospel truths that unite and strengthen. Leaders, entrusted with stewardship over God's flock, are called to embody Christ's sacrificial love and humility, guiding the faithful with compassion and wisdom.

Rediscovering Intimacy with Christ

At its core, the narrative of the runaway bride invites introspection and renewal. It calls the Church to rediscover intimacy with Christ, not through legalism or authoritarianism but through a profound communion grounded in love and grace. As leaders and believers alike heed this call, they participate in the unfolding story of redemption and renewal, where the Church, as the radiant bride, stands steadfast in her devotion to her bridegroom, Christ.

The Runaway Bride: Straying from the Divine Calling

A Call to Fidelity

The essence of the Church, likened to the Bride of Christ, is rooted in fidelity, purity, and unwavering commitment to the teachings of her divine spouse. Yet, across the annals of history and within contemporary times, cracks in this fidelity have appeared. These fissures, born of human frailty, misguidance, and demonic activity, threaten to obscure the Church's radiant identity and compromise its sacred mission.

Challenges to Fidelity

Throughout history, the Church has faced myriads of challenges to its fidelity. From doctrinal disputes and political entanglements to moral failings and internal strife, each challenge has tested the Church's resolve to remain true to Christ's teachings. These moments of fracture, though painful, serve as opportunities for introspection and renewal, prompting the faithful to reaffirm their commitment to the unchanging truths of the gospel.

The Impact of Compromise

When fidelity wanes, the Church risks losing its moral authority and spiritual influence. Compromise with cultural norms or succumbing to the allure of power can lead to a dilution of its message and a distortion of its purpose. The bride, intended to shine as a beacon of truth and grace, becomes ensnared in the complexities of human ambition and earthly pursuits. Yet, amidst the shadows of compromise, there exists a path to renewal and restoration. Just as Hosea prophesied God's relentless pursuit of His people, so too does Christ beckon His Church to return to Him with hearts renewed and spirits revived. This call to fidelity is not merely a call for adherence to rules but a beckoning to embrace the transformative power of grace and truth.

Embracing True Unity

True unity within the Church emerges not from uniformity of opinion or compliance with external standards but from a shared commitment to Christ and His gospel. It is found in humility, mutual respect, and a willingness to seek reconciliation where division has taken root. Leaders, as stewards of this unity, bear a solemn responsibility to shepherd with integrity and grace, fostering an environment where love and truth flourish.

Leadership and the Disruption of Unity

Leadership within the Church holds a sacred responsibility to guide and nurture, yet all too often, the allure of power and human frailty disrupts this mandate. Instead of shepherding the flock with humility and wisdom, some leaders wield authority with a heavy hand, causing dissent and fragmentation.

The Sacred Trust of Leadership

At its core, leadership within the Church is a sacred trust bestowed upon individuals to steward the spiritual well-being of the community. This trust is not rooted in hierarchical supremacy but in service and sacrificial love, mirroring Christ's example of servant leadership. Leaders are entrusted with the solemn duty to nourish the faith of believers, providing spiritual guidance and support in times of joy and adversity alike.

The Allure of Power and Human Frailty

However, the path of leadership is fraught with temptations. The allure of power, whether through influence, control, or recognition, can subtly erode the noble intentions of even the most well-meaning leaders. Human frailty further complicates this landscape, as personal ambition, pride, and insecurities can cloud judgment and lead to decisions that prioritize self-interest over the welfare of the flock.

Wielding Authority with a Heavy Hand

When leaders succumb to these temptations, the consequences reverberate throughout the Church community. Instead of fostering unity and nurturing spiritual growth, they may assert authority with a heavy hand, imposing rigid doctrines or silencing opposing voices. This approach, while seemingly authoritative, often breeds resentment and alienation among the faithful, fracturing the unity that Christ intended for His body.

Causes of Dissent and Fragmentation

Dissent and fragmentation within the Church can stem from various causes, but a significant factor is the mishandling of leadership authority. When leaders prioritize control over compassion, conformity over diversity of thought, or institutional preservation over spiritual renewal, they risk alienating segments of the congregation. This can lead to disillusionment among the faithful, weakening the Church's collective witness and diminishing its effectiveness in fulfilling its mission.

A Call to Humility and Servant Leadership

In response to these challenges, the Church is called to reaffirm the principles of humility and servant leadership. True, spiritual authority is not asserted through dominance but demonstrated through humility, empathy, and a commitment to the well-being of all believers. Leaders must cultivate a spirit of openness to diverse perspectives, fostering dialogue and collaboration rather than enforcing rigid orthodoxy.

Embodying Christ-like Leadership

Christ, as the ultimate example of leadership, embodied humility and sacrificial love in His ministry. He washed the feet of His disciples and laid down His life for the redemption of humanity. Likewise, leaders within the Church are called to emulate His example, prioritizing the spiritual nourishment and unity of the flock above personal agendas or institutional interests.

The Runaway Train of Dissension

Imagine a runaway train hurtling down the tracks, unchecked and out of control. This metaphor mirrors the state of the Church when leadership fails in its sacred duty. Dissension spreads like wildfire among the flock, weakening the Church's moral authority and spiritual unity.

Consequences of Spiritual Disarray

When the Church deviates from its divine calling, the consequences reverberate widely. Spiritual disarray diminishes the Church's ability to offer solace and guidance to a world in need. The faithful, likened to bewildered sheep, seek direction but find themselves wandering in confusion as the clarity of purpose dims.

Rediscovering the Path

Amidst the turmoil, there remains hope. The narrative of the runaway bride is not one of finality but of redemption and renewal. By returning to the foundational principles of love, grace, and humility, the Church can reclaim its role as the radiant bride eagerly anticipating her groom.

True leadership within the Church must embrace humility and servanthood, embodying the example set forth by Christ himself. Through transparency, accountability, and a steadfast commitment to truth, leaders can repair the breaches and restore unity among the faithful.

Abounding Grace and Forgiveness

Central to the metaphor of the Bride of Christ is the theme of grace—undeserved favor extended freely by God to humanity. Ephesians 2:8-9 encapsulates this truth: "For it is by grace you have been saved, through faith—and this is not from yourselves, it is the gift of God—not by works, so that no one can boast." Christ's sacrificial love on the cross is the ultimate expression of this grace, where He redeems and reconciles us to Himself, offering forgiveness for sins and the promise of eternal life.

As the Bride of Christ, we are invited into a journey of restoration and transformation. Christ's love does not leave us unchanged but works within us to heal our brokenness and transform us into His likeness. Romans 12:2

exhorts believers to be transformed by the renewing of their minds, embracing God's will and His perfect plan for their lives.

The metaphor of the Church as the Bride of Christ beautifully encapsulates the dynamic relationship between Christ and His people. Through His pursuit, grace, and transformative love, Christ restores and redeems His Church, shaping us into a radiant and pure Bride. As we embrace this redemptive journey, individually and collectively, we testify to the world of God's unfailing love and His power to bring healing and transformation. May we continually yield to His refining work, eagerly anticipating the day when we will be presented to Him, blameless and without blemish, at the wedding feast of the Lamb.

The path to healing and renewal within the Church begins with a reaffirmation of authentic leadership characterized by humility and compassion. By acknowledging and addressing the pitfalls of power and human frailty, leaders can foster an environment where trust is restored, unity is strengthened, and the Church can fulfill its calling as the radiant Bride of Christ, reflecting His love and grace to a world in need.

Leading God's People According to the Bible

By Dr. Sherley Lefevre

(All scriptures were taken from the New International Version of the Bible)

I chose to write this chapter on leadership God's way because it is crucial to revisit and understand the biblical principles that God has laid out for leading His people. In today's world, we often witness churches straying from these divine guidelines, resulting in harm to their congregations. By returning to the foundational teachings of the Bible, we can rediscover the true essence of godly leadership and ensure that the flock is nurtured and protected according to God's will.

This chapter is an urgent call to Christian ministers, teachers, and leaders with the divine blueprint for leadership. As we delve into the Scriptures, we uncover timeless wisdom and transformative examples that illuminate the path to effective and compassionate leadership. In a time when many church leaders are swayed by secular ideals and personal ambitions, it's more important than ever to anchor our leadership in the enduring truths of the Bible. Through this exploration, I aim to inspire a revival of authentic, Christ-centered leadership that truly reflects God's heart for His people and restores the church to its intended role as a lighthouse of integrity and love in the world.

Leadership within the Christian context is fundamentally different from secular leadership due to its divine orientation and spiritual foundation. Effective leadership of God's people is rooted in the teachings and examples found in the Bible. This chapter explores biblical principles and models of leadership, emphasizing the qualities and practices that contribute to leading God's people effectively. If you are in any capacity to lead God's children within the church institution, then this chapter is for you.

The Foundation of Biblical Leadership

The Call to Serve

The concept of leadership in the Bible is closely tied to servanthood. Jesus Christ Himself exemplified servant leadership, as seen in His words in Matthew 20:28: "Just as the Son of Man did not come to be served, but to serve, and to give his life as a ransom for many." Effective leaders are those who prioritize the needs of others, placing service above self-interest.

In the biblical context, servanthood is not merely an act of humility but a profound demonstration of love and commitment to others. Jesus' life and ministry were a continuous testament to this principle. He washed His disciples' feet (John 13:1-17), a task typically reserved for the lowest of servants, to teach them that true greatness lies in serving others selflessly. This act was a powerful reminder that leaders must be willing to perform even the most menial tasks for the sake of their followers.

Moreover, the Bible repeatedly emphasizes that leaders are stewards of God's people. They are entrusted with the well-being of their flock and are accountable to God for how they fulfill this role. In 1 Peter 5:2-3, leaders are exhorted to "Be shepherds of God's flock that is under your care, watching over them—not because you must, but because you are willing, as God wants you to be; not pursuing dishonest gain, but eager to serve; not lording it over those entrusted to you, but being examples to the flock." This passage underscores that leadership is a voluntary act of service, motivated by love and a genuine desire to care for others, rather than a pursuit of power or personal gain.

Servant leadership also involves empowering others. Jesus invested in His disciples, equipping them with the knowledge and skills needed to continue His work. He sent them out to preach, heal, and serve, thereby extending His ministry through them (Luke 9:1-6). Similarly, modern biblical leaders are called to mentor and develop their followers, enabling them to grow in their faith and contribute to the community.

In essence, biblical servanthood transforms the conventional notion of leadership. It shifts the focus from authority and control to compassion, humility, and a steadfast commitment to the well-being of others. Leaders who embrace this model create environments where individuals feel valued, supported, and inspired to live out their God-given potential. By following Jesus' example of servant leadership, we fulfill our divine calling and reflect God's love and grace in our leadership practices.

Character Traits of Biblical Leaders

The character traits of godly leadership are deeply rooted in the fruit of the Spirit, as outlined in Galatians 5:22-23: "But the fruit of the Spirit is love, joy, peace, forbearance, kindness, goodness, faithfulness, gentleness, and self-control." A godly leader embodies these attributes, creating a foundation of integrity and trustworthiness. Love is paramount, as it drives a leader's compassion and genuine care for their people. Joy and peace provide stability and optimism, even in challenging times. Forbearance, or patience, is essential in guiding others with understanding and grace. Kindness and goodness reflect the leader's desire to do what is right and beneficial for others. Faithfulness denotes a steadfast commitment to God and His principles, while gentleness ensures that leaders approach others with humility and respect. Finally, self-control is crucial for maintaining discipline and setting a positive example. Together, these traits enable leaders to serve effectively, build strong relationships, and inspire others to follow God's path.

Integrity and Righteousness

A key characteristic of biblical leaders is integrity. Proverbs 11:3 states, "The integrity of the upright guides them, but the unfaithful are destroyed by their duplicity." Leaders must be honest, transparent, and morally upright, guiding their followers by example. Righteousness involves living by God's standards, as seen in Noah, who was described as "a righteous man, blameless among the people of his time, and he walked faithfully with God" (Genesis 6:9). Integrity also encompasses consistency between one's beliefs and actions, ensuring that there is no disparity between what a leader preaches and practices.

Moreover, integrity builds trust and credibility, essential for any effective leadership. When leaders consistently demonstrate integrity, they earn the respect and confidence of those they lead, fostering an environment of trust and security. This trust enables a leader to influence and inspire others positively, as followers are more likely to emulate the leader's example.

Integrity is further highlighted in the life of Daniel, who remained steadfast in his faith and principles despite the pressures of a foreign culture and the threat of persecution. Daniel's refusal to compromise his values, even when faced with the lions' den (Daniel 6), exemplifies the unwavering commitment to righteousness that godly leadership demands. His integrity not only protected him but also led to the glorification of God among the nations.

Additionally, integrity in leadership involves accountability. Leaders who practice integrity are open to correction and willing to admit their mistakes, seeking forgiveness and making amends where necessary. King David, despite his significant failures, is a prime example of this trait. His heartfelt repentance and plea for God's mercy in Psalm 51 reveal a leader who, despite his flaws, was sincere in his desire to align his life with God's will.

Integrity is the cornerstone of godly leadership. It requires unwavering adherence to truth, transparency, and moral uprightness. By embodying integrity, leaders not only honor God but also create a solid foundation for leading others with authenticity, earning their trust, and guiding them in righteousness.

The Role of Prayer and Dependence on God

Seeking God's Guidance

Effective leaders prioritize prayer, seeking God's wisdom and direction. James 1:5 encourages believers to ask for wisdom, and leaders must continually seek divine guidance. Jesus Himself often withdrew to pray (Luke 5:16), modeling a life dependent on the Father. Leaders must cultivate a disciplined prayer life, interceding for their people and seeking God's plans.

Prayer is not merely a ritual but a vital communication channel with God, through which leaders gain clarity, strength, and discernment. It is in the quiet moments of prayer that leaders can hear God's voice, receive His comfort, and be filled with His peace. The Apostle Paul emphasizes the importance of constant prayer, urging believers to "pray without ceasing" (1 Thessalonians 5:17). This continuous dialogue with God ensures that leaders remain aligned with His will and purposes.

Moreover, prayer is a powerful tool for intercession. Leaders are called to stand in the gap for their people, lifting their needs, struggles, and victories before God. Moses' intercession for Israel (Exodus 32:11-14) and Daniel's fervent prayers for his nation (Daniel 9:3-19) illustrate the profound impact of a leader's prayers on the well-being of their community. Through intercessory prayer, leaders express their love and concern for their flock, seeking God's intervention and blessings on their behalf.

A disciplined prayer life also fosters humility and dependence on God. Recognizing that true wisdom and guidance come from the Lord, effective leaders continually surrender their plans and decisions to Him. This dependence is exemplified in King Solomon, who, when given the opportunity to ask for anything, chose to seek wisdom from God to lead His people rightly (1 Kings 3:7-9). Solomon's example underscores the importance of seeking God's wisdom above all else in leadership.

Additionally, prayer equips leaders to face challenges and spiritual battles. Ephesians 6:18 advises believers to "pray in the Spirit on all occasions with all kinds of prayers and requests." Through prayer, leaders receive the spiritual fortitude needed to withstand opposition, overcome obstacles, and lead with courage and conviction. Jesus' prayers in the Garden of Gethsemane (Matthew 26:36-46) before His crucifixion reveal the strength and resolve that comes from seeking the Father's will in times of great trial.

Overall, prayer is the lifeblood of effective, godly leadership. It is through prayer that leaders connect with God, gain His wisdom, intercede for their people, and receive the strength to fulfill their calling. By prioritizing a disciplined prayer life, leaders demonstrate their reliance on God and their commitment to leading His people according to His divine direction.

Effective leadership of God's people is deeply rooted in biblical principles and examples. It requires a foundation of servanthood, divine calling, and integrity. Biblical leaders must demonstrate humility, courage, and dependence on God through prayer. Articulating a clear vision, implementing strategic plans, fostering discipleship, managing conflicts, and emphasizing ethical leadership are essential practices. Ultimately, effective leadership is about guiding God's people with a heart aligned with His, ensuring their spiritual growth and well-being, and advancing God's kingdom purposes.

In leading God's people, we look to the ultimate example of Jesus Christ, the Good Shepherd, who laid down His life for His sheep. By following His example and adhering to biblical principles, leaders can effectively shepherd God's flock, bringing glory to Him and blessing His people.

Shepherding God's People According to the Bible

Shepherding God's people is a central theme throughout the Bible, reflecting God's care and guidance for His followers. The role of a shepherd is metaphorically applied to leaders, pastors, and those responsible for the spiritual well-being of others. In biblical times, a shepherd's primary role was to care for and protect the sheep. This concept extends to spiritual leadership, where shepherds are called to nurture, guide, and safeguard their flock. Psalm 23 beautifully illustrates God as the ultimate shepherd who provides, guides, and protects: "The Lord is my shepherd; I shall not want. He makes me lie down in green pastures. He leads me beside still waters. He restores my soul" (Psalm 23:1-3).

Jesus as the Good Shepherd

Jesus Christ identifies Himself as the Good Shepherd in John 10:11, saying, "I am the good shepherd. The good shepherd lays down his life for the sheep." This declaration sets the standard for shepherding, emphasizing sacrificial love, commitment, and the willingness to lay down one's life for the well-being of the flock. Jesus' model of shepherding is one of intimate knowledge of His sheep and their needs, leading with compassion and selflessness.

Qualities of a Good Shepherd

Compassion and Love

A good shepherd is characterized by compassion and love for the flock. Jesus exemplified this in His ministry, showing deep compassion for the multitudes (Matthew 9:36). Compassion drives a shepherd to go to great lengths to care for and rescue the sheep, as illustrated in the parable of the lost sheep (Luke 15:4-7). Shepherds must genuinely care for the spiritual, emotional, and physical needs of those they lead.

Wisdom and Discernment

Wisdom and discernment are vital for shepherding. Shepherds must navigate complex spiritual and practical issues, making decisions that impact the well-being of their flock. James 1:5 encourages leaders to seek wisdom from God: "If any of you lacks wisdom, you should ask God, who gives generously to all without finding fault, and it will be given to you." Discernment helps shepherds recognize the needs of their flock and the right course of action.

Responsibilities of a Shepherd

Feeding the Flock

One of the primary responsibilities of a shepherd is to feed the flock. Spiritually, this involves teaching and preaching the Word of God. Jesus instructed Peter, "Feed my lambs" and "Take care of my sheep" (John 21:15-17), emphasizing the importance of providing spiritual nourishment. Shepherds must diligently study and teach the Scriptures, ensuring their flock is grounded in biblical truth.

Guiding and Leading

Shepherds are called to guide and lead their flock. Psalm 23:3-4 illustrates the shepherd's role in leading the sheep along the right paths and through dark valleys. Effective shepherds provide clear direction, helping their flock navigate life's challenges and make godly decisions. Proverbs 3:5-6 encourages believers to trust in the Lord's guidance, and shepherds play a key role in pointing their flock towards God's path.

Protecting and Watching Over

Protecting the flock from spiritual dangers is a crucial responsibility. Shepherds must be vigilant, as Paul warned the Ephesian elders: "Keep watch over yourselves and all the flock of which the Holy Spirit has made you overseers. Be shepherds of the church of God" (Acts 20:28). This involves guarding against false teachings, sin, and any threat to the spiritual well-being of the flock.

Biblical Examples of Shepherding

Moses: Leading with Patience and Perseverance

Moses is a quintessential example of a shepherd leader. Despite his initial reluctance, Moses led the Israelites out of Egypt and through the wilderness with patience and perseverance. His leadership involved interceding for the people (Exodus 32:11-14), teaching them God's laws (Exodus 20), and dealing with their complaints and rebellion (Numbers 14). Moses' example highlights the importance of endurance, intercession, and teaching in shepherding.

David: Shepherding with a Heart for God

David's background as a shepherd uniquely equipped him to lead Israel. His psalms reflect his deep reliance on God and his shepherd's heart. David's leadership was marked by his desire to serve God and his people, as seen in his care for Mephibosheth (2 Samuel 9) and his efforts to unify the kingdom (2 Samuel 5). David's life demonstrates the significance of a heart aligned with God's purposes in effective shepherding.

Dr. Sherley Lefevre, Ph.D.

Problems with Leadership in the Church Today

Leadership within the church is intended to reflect Christ's love, humility, and servanthood. However, contemporary church leadership is often plagued by serious issues that deviate from these biblical principles. Manipulation, control, spiritual abuse, false teachings, and other unethical practices have infiltrated many churches, causing significant harm to congregations and tarnishing the church's witness to the world. Here, we explore these problems in detail:

1. Manipulation and Control

Manipulation and control are pervasive issues in some church leadership structures. Leaders may use their authority to manipulate congregants into compliance or to achieve personal agendas. This can manifest in various ways, such as emotional manipulation, coercive tactics, and exploiting people's vulnerabilities to maintain power and influence. Such behavior is contrary to the servant leadership model that Jesus exemplified, where leaders are called to serve and uplift their flock, not to dominate them. In contrast to this abusive behavior, Peter exhorts leaders to "be shepherds of God's flock...not lording it over those entrusted to you but being examples to the flock" (1 Peter 5:2-3).

2. Spiritual Abuse

Spiritual abuse occurs when leaders misuse their spiritual authority to control, manipulate, or harm congregants. This abuse can be subtle or overt, and it often leaves deep emotional and spiritual scars. Victims of spiritual abuse may feel isolated, guilty, and fearful, as their faith and trust are exploited. This can lead to a distorted understanding of God and a damaged relationship with Him. The Bible warns against this kind of leadership in Ezekiel 34, where God condemns the shepherds of Israel for exploiting the flock instead of caring for them: "You have ruled them harshly and brutally" (Ezekiel 34:4).

3. False Teachings and Bad Doctrine

False teachings and bad doctrine pose significant threats to the spiritual health of the church. Leaders who deviate from sound biblical teaching can lead their congregants astray, promoting beliefs and practices that are contrary to Scripture. This can result from a lack of theological training, intentional deception, or the desire to cater to popular opinion rather than adhering to biblical truth. Paul warned Timothy about this danger, urging him to "Preach the word; be prepared in season and out of season; correct, rebuke and encourage—with great patience and careful instruction. For the time will come when people will not put up with sound doctrine" (2 Timothy 4:2-3).

4. Witchcraft and Superstition

In some cases, church leaders incorporate elements of witchcraft, superstition, or unbiblical rituals into their practices. This can involve the use of charms, incantations, or other forms of spiritual manipulation to exert control over congregants. Such practices are explicitly condemned in Scripture as detestable to God. Deuteronomy 18:10-12 states, "Let no one be found among you who...practices divination or sorcery, interprets omens, engages in witchcraft...Anyone who does these things is detestable to the Lord." The introduction of these elements into church practice can lead believers away from the true worship of God and create a culture of fear and superstition.

5. Abuse of Power and Authority

Abuse of power and authority is another critical issue in church leadership. Some leaders use their position to exploit others for personal gain, whether financially, sexually, or otherwise. This can create an environment of fear and oppression, where congregants feel powerless to speak out or seek help. The Bible calls for leaders to be "above reproach, faithful to his wife, temperate, self-controlled, respectable, hospitable, able to teach, not given to drunkenness, not violent but gentle, not quarrelsome, not a lover of money" (1 Timothy 3:2-3). Leaders who fail to embody these qualities bring disrepute to the church and cause immeasurable harm to individuals and communities.

6. Lack of Accountability and Transparency

A lack of accountability and transparency within church leadership often leads to unchecked misconduct and abuse. Without proper structures to hold leaders accountable, there is a risk of corruption, financial mismanagement, and moral failure. Churches must establish systems of governance that ensure leaders are accountable to their congregations and higher ecclesiastical authorities. Paul's instruction to the Corinthians highlights the importance of transparency: "For we are taking pains to do what is right, not only in the eyes of the Lord but also in the eyes of man" (2 Corinthians 8:21).

7. Authoritarian Leadership Styles

Authoritarian leadership styles, where leaders rule with an iron fist and tolerate no dissent, are also problematic. This approach blocks dialogue, suppresses differing viewpoints, and can lead to a culture of fear and conformity rather than one of growth and spiritual maturity. Healthy leadership should encourage open communication, foster a spirit of collaboration, and create an environment where congregants feel valued and heard. Jesus' model of leadership was one of humility and servanthood, not authoritarian control: "Whoever wants to become great among you must be your servant, and whoever wants to be first must be slave of all" (Mark 10:43-44).

The issues of manipulation, control, spiritual abuse, false teachings, witchcraft, abuse of power, lack of accountability, and authoritarian leadership in the church are serious and pervasive. These problems not only harm individuals but also damage the church's witness and mission. Addressing these issues requires a return to biblical principles of leadership, characterized by integrity, humility, servanthood, accountability, and a deep commitment to God's truth. By realigning church leadership with these biblical standards, the church can restore its role as a beacon of hope, love, and righteousness in a broken world. Shepherding God's people is a sacred and significant responsibility, deeply rooted in biblical principles and examples. A good shepherd cares for, guides, and protects the flock with compassion, integrity, and wisdom.

Narcissism within the Church Walls

By Dr. Sherley Lefevre

(All scriptures were taken from the New International Version of the Bible)

During my 26-year journey as a Christian, I have encountered a variety of leadership styles and personalities within the church. Among them, the most detrimental and toxic has been the narcissistic leader. This type of leader often exhibits a profound sense of entitlement, prioritizing personal glory over the well-being of the congregation. Their leadership is characterized by manipulation, a lack of empathy, and a tendency to exploit others for their own gain.

Narcissistic leaders can create an environment of fear, control, and division within the church community. They may hinder opposition, undermine healthy relationships, and alienate those who do not conform to their desires or beliefs. Their charismatic facade can initially attract followers, but over time, their self-serving behaviors can lead to spiritual disillusionment and the erosion of trust among church members.

In my experience, navigating under a narcissistic leader has highlighted the importance of discernment, accountability structures, and a commitment to biblical principles of humility and servant leadership. It underscores the need for churches to prioritize transparency, genuine care for others, and collective spiritual growth over individual ambitions and ego-driven agendas.

Narcissism, characterized by an inflated sense of self-importance and a deep need for admiration, can have a profound impact on relationships and leadership within any community. When it infiltrates the Christian sector and church walls, the consequences can be particularly damaging. This chapter explores the nature of narcissism, its effects on relationships and leadership within the church, and what the Bible says about this issue. We will also discuss strategies for overcoming narcissism and its impact on congregants.

Understanding Narcissism

Narcissism is a personality disorder that manifests in grandiosity, a lack of empathy, and a need for excessive admiration. Individuals with narcissistic tendencies often prioritize their own needs and desires over those of others, leading to strained relationships and dysfunctional environments. In the context of the church, narcissistic behavior can disrupt the unity and spiritual growth of the congregation. Such individuals may dominate conversations, seek constant validation, and undermine the contributions of others, creating a toxic atmosphere. This behavior can erode trust and hinder collaborative efforts, ultimately compromising the church's mission and community cohesion. Furthermore, narcissistic leaders within religious settings may exploit their positions for personal gain or glory, manipulating the faith and trust of their followers. Their charismatic facade can mask a profound lack of genuine empathy and commitment to the well-being of the congregation, potentially leading to spiritual disillusionment and division among believers. Thus, addressing and mitigating narcissistic behavior is crucial for fostering a healthy and harmonious religious community focused on collective spiritual growth and mutual support.

Narcissism in Relationships

Personal Relationships

Narcissism can severely affect personal relationships within the church community. Narcissistic individuals often struggle with genuine empathy, making it difficult for them to form and maintain healthy relationships. They may:

- **Manipulate others**: Narcissists often use manipulation to maintain control over their relationships. They may employ tactics such as gaslighting, guilt-tripping, and exploiting vulnerabilities to keep others in a submissive position.

- **Lack of empathy**: A hallmark of narcissism is the inability to empathize with others. This can lead to insensitive or hurtful behavior, as the narcissist may not recognize or care about the emotional needs of others.

- **Seek admiration**: Narcissists crave constant validation and admiration. In relationships, this can manifest as a need to be the center of attention, often at the expense of others' feelings and needs.

In a church setting, professional relationships between clergy, staff, and congregants can also be affected by narcissistic behavior. Narcissistic leaders may:

- **Create a toxic environment**: Narcissistic leaders often foster a climate of fear and competition rather than one of cooperation and mutual support. This can lead to high turnover rates among staff and a general sense of dissatisfaction within the church.

- **Undermine teamwork**: Teamwork and collaboration are essential in any organization, including the church. Narcissistic leaders, however, may undermine these efforts by taking credit for others' work, refusing to delegate, and prioritizing their agendas over the collective good.

Narcissism in Leadership

Leadership within the church carries significant responsibility. Leaders are expected to shepherd their congregations, provide spiritual guidance, and model Christ-like behavior. Narcissistic traits in leaders can severely hinder their ability to fulfill these roles effectively.

Characteristics of Narcissistic Leaders

Narcissistic leaders often exhibit the following characteristics:

- **Authoritarianism**: Narcissistic leaders tend to adopt an authoritarian style, demanding unquestioning obedience and punishing dissent. This can stifle open dialogue and critical thinking within the congregation.

- **Exploitation**: These leaders may exploit their position for personal gain, whether that be financial, social, or emotional. They may use their authority to manipulate and control others, rather than serving and uplifting them.

- **Lack of Accountability**: Narcissistic leaders often resist accountability, refusing to acknowledge mistakes or accept constructive criticism. This can lead to a lack of transparency and integrity within the church.

Impact on the Congregation

The presence of narcissistic leaders can have profound and far-reaching effects on the congregation:

- **Erosion of Trust**: Trust is fundamental to any healthy community. Narcissistic behavior can erode trust between leaders and congregants, leading to a breakdown in relationships and a fragmented church community.

- **Spiritual Harm**: When leaders prioritize their own needs over the spiritual well-being of their congregants, it can lead to spiritual harm. Congregants may feel neglected, manipulated, or spiritually abused, which can hinder their faith journey.

- **Inhibition of Growth**: A narcissistic leader's focus on self-promotion can inhibit the overall growth of the church. Instead of fostering a culture of discipleship and spiritual growth, the leader's actions may stifle these vital aspects of church life.

Biblical Perspective on Narcissism

The Bible provides clear guidance on the qualities and behaviors expected of leaders and believers, many of whom stand in direct opposition to narcissistic tendencies.

Humility and Servanthood

The Bible repeatedly emphasizes the importance of humility and servanthood. Jesus Himself is the ultimate example of these virtues:

- **Philippians 2:3-4**: "Do nothing out of selfish ambition or vain conceit. Rather, in humility value others above yourselves, not looking to your own interests but each of you to the interests of the others."

- **Matthew 20:26-28**: "Not so with you. Instead, whoever wants to become great among you must be your servant, and whoever wants to be first must be your slave—just as the Son of Man did not come to be served, but to serve, and to give his life as a ransom for many."

These passages underscore the need for leaders and believers to adopt a posture of humility and servanthood, prioritizing the needs of others over their desires for power and recognition.

Love and Empathy

Love and empathy are central to the Christian faith. The Bible calls believers to love one another deeply and to show compassion:

- **John 13:34-35**: "A new command I give you: Love one another. As I have loved you, so you must love one another. By this everyone will know that you are my disciples, if you love one another."

- **Colossians 3:12**: "Therefore, as God's chosen people, holy and dearly loved, clothe yourselves with compassion, kindness, humility, gentleness and patience."

These verses highlight the importance of genuine love and empathy in fostering healthy relationships within the church.

Integrity and Accountability

The Bible also emphasizes the importance of integrity and accountability in leadership:

- **1 Timothy 3:2-3**: "Now the overseer is to be above reproach, faithful to his wife, temperate, self-controlled, respectable, hospitable, able to teach, not given to drunkenness, not violent but gentle, not quarrelsome, not a lover of money."

- **James 3:1**: "Not many of you should become teachers, my fellow believers, because you know that we who teach will be judged more strictly."

These passages remind leaders of the high standards of conduct expected of them and the need for accountability in their actions, emphasizing that leadership in the church is a sacred responsibility entrusted by God, requiring humility, integrity, and a genuine commitment to serving others with love and compassion. Leaders are called to emulate Christ's example of selflessness and sacrificial love, putting the needs of the community above their ambitions or desires.

Overcoming Narcissism

Addressing narcissism within the church requires a multifaceted approach, involving personal reflection, communal support, and systemic changes. Individual reflection encourages self-awareness and accountability, prompting those with narcissistic tendencies to recognize and address their behavior. Communal support entails fostering an environment where open dialogue and healthy relationships are prioritized, encouraging empathy and mutual respect among members. Systemic changes involve implementing clear guidelines and accountability structures within church leadership, ensuring transparency and ethical conduct. By promoting humility, empathy, and a shared commitment to spiritual values, churches can cultivate a culture of authenticity and collective well-being, mitigating the harmful effects of narcissism and fostering a nurturing spiritual community.

Personal Reflection and Growth

For individuals struggling with narcissistic tendencies, personal reflection and growth are crucial:

- **Self-awareness**: Developing self-awareness is the first step toward overcoming narcissism. This involves recognizing and acknowledging narcissistic traits and understanding their impact on others.

- **Repentance**: In the Christian context, repentance is essential. This means genuinely turning away from selfish behaviors and seeking forgiveness from those who have been hurt.

- **Counseling and Support**: Professional counseling, particularly from a Christian counselor, can provide valuable insights and strategies for managing narcissistic tendencies.

Communal Support and Accountability

The church community plays a vital role in supporting individuals and leaders in overcoming narcissism:

- **Fostering a culture of accountability**: Establishing systems of accountability within the church can help prevent narcissistic behavior from taking root. This might include regular performance reviews, peer feedback, and transparent decision-making processes.

- **Encouraging vulnerability and openness**: Creating a safe space for vulnerability and openness can help individuals feel more comfortable addressing their struggles. This can be facilitated through small groups, mentorship programs, and pastoral care.

- **Promoting servant leadership**: Emphasizing the values of servant leadership can help counteract narcissistic tendencies. Leaders should be encouraged to prioritize the needs of their congregants and to model humility and service.

The Role of the Congregation

Congregants also have a responsibility in addressing and mitigating the effects of narcissism within the church:

- **Discernment and Prayer**: Congregants should seek discernment and pray for their leaders, asking God to reveal any harmful behaviors and to guide their leaders toward humility and integrity.

- **Speaking the Truth in Love**: When witnessing narcissistic behavior, congregants should approach the situation with love and care, addressing their concerns respectfully and constructively.

- **Supporting Healthy Leadership**: By actively supporting and encouraging healthy leadership practices, congregants can help foster a positive and nurturing church environment.

Biblical Examples of Narcissists

To further understand the impact of narcissism and how it manifests, we can look at several biblical figures who exhibited narcissistic traits. These examples provide valuable lessons on the consequences of such behavior and reinforce the importance of humility, repentance, and genuine leadership.

King Saul

King Saul, the first king of Israel, is a prime example of a leader whose narcissistic traits led to his downfall. Initially chosen by God, Saul started his reign with promise but soon exhibited behaviors that reflected his insecurity, jealousy, and need for admiration.

1 Samuel 15:10-12: "Then the word of the Lord came to Samuel: 'I regret that I have made Saul king, because he has turned away from me and has not carried out my instructions.' Samuel was angry, and he cried out to the Lord all that night. Early in the morning Samuel got up and went to meet Saul, but he was told, 'Saul has gone to Carmel. There he has set up a monument in his own honor and has turned and gone on down to Gilgal.'"

Saul's actions, such as setting up a monument in his own honor, reflect his need for personal glory and recognition. His inability to accept David's rising popularity led to irrational jealousy and paranoia, ultimately contributing to his downfall.

1 Samuel 18:7-9: "As they danced, they sang: 'Saul has slain his thousands, and David his tens of thousands.' Saul was very angry; this refrain displeased him greatly. 'They have credited David with tens of thousands,' he thought, 'but me with only thousands. What more can he get but the kingdom?' And from that time on Saul kept a close eye on David."

Saul's jealousy of David's success and the people's admiration for David further exemplifies his narcissistic traits. Instead of celebrating the victories that benefited his kingdom, Saul saw David as a threat to his status and power.

King Nebuchadnezzar

King Nebuchadnezzar of Babylon is another biblical figure who displayed narcissistic behavior. His story is a powerful illustration of the dangers of pride and the importance of humility.

Daniel 4:29-30: "Twelve months later, as the king was walking on the roof of the royal palace of Babylon, he said, 'Is not this the great Babylon I have built as the royal residence, by my mighty power and for the glory of my majesty?'"

Nebuchadnezzar's statement reflects his belief in his superiority and his desire for personal glory. This self-centered perspective led to his downfall, as God humbled him by causing him to lose his sanity temporarily.

Daniel 4:31-32: "Even as the words were on his lips, a voice came from heaven, 'This is what is decreed for you, King Nebuchadnezzar: Your royal authority has been taken from you. You will be driven away from people and will live with the wild animals; you will eat grass like the ox. Seven times will pass by for you until you acknowledge that the Most High is sovereign over all kingdoms on earth and gives them to anyone he wishes.'"

Nebuchadnezzar's eventual repentance and acknowledgment of God's sovereignty illustrate the possibility of redemption even for those with deeply narcissistic traits.

Diotrephes

In the New Testament, Diotrephes is mentioned as a church leader who exhibited narcissistic behavior. His actions and attitudes disrupted the unity and functioning of the early Christian community.

3 John 1:9-10: "I wrote to the church, but Diotrephes, who loves to be first, will not welcome us. So when I come, I will call attention to what he is doing, spreading malicious nonsense about us. Not satisfied with that, he even refuses to welcome other believers. He also stops those who want to do so and puts them out of the church."

Diotrephes' desire to be first and his refusal to welcome other believers demonstrate his self-centeredness and need for control. His behavior created division within the church and hindered the mission of the early Christians.

Lessons from Biblical Narcissists

The stories of Saul, Nebuchadnezzar, and Diotrephes offer several important lessons for contemporary Christians:

The Consequences of Pride

These biblical examples show that pride and self-centeredness can lead to severe consequences. Saul lost his kingdom, Nebuchadnezzar lost his sanity, and Diotrephes caused division within the church. These outcomes illustrate the destructive power of narcissism and the importance of humility. Saul's jealousy and disobedience led to his downfall, Nebuchadnezzar's pride brought about a period of madness until he humbled himself before God, and Diotrephes' desire for preeminence led him to reject apostolic authority and sow discord among believers. These historical narratives serve as cautionary tales, emphasizing the enduring relevance of humility and servant leadership in fostering spiritual health and unity within religious communities.

The Need for Accountability

Each of these figures lacked proper accountability, which allowed their narcissistic behaviors to flourish. In the case of Saul, his unchecked jealousy and disobedience went unchallenged, leading to disastrous consequences for himself and his kingdom. Nebuchadnezzar's unchecked pride led to a period of madness until he acknowledged his dependence on God. Diotrephes' desire for preeminence in the early church caused division because he resisted accountability to apostolic authority.

In the church today, systems of accountability can help prevent such behaviors from taking root and causing harm. Transparent decision-making processes ensure that leaders are held accountable for their actions and decisions. Having systems in place where decisions are made collectively instead of by one individual can be very beneficial. An environment where feedback is encouraged and valued allows concerns about narcissistic behaviors to be addressed promptly, promoting transparency and trust among church members. By implementing these accountability measures, churches can uphold ethical standards, safeguard against abuses of power, and cultivate a community where humility and service are esteemed over personal ambition and pride.

To address and overcome narcissism within the church, it is essential to apply the lessons learned from the previous biblical examples. Furthermore, some additional ways in which leaders can tackle the issue of narcissism in the church are to:

1. **Cultivate Humility**: Encourage humility by fostering a culture where servanthood is valued over self-promotion. Leaders should model humility in their actions and attitudes.

2. **Promote Accountability**: Establish robust systems of accountability within the church. This includes open communication channels and mechanisms for congregants to voice concerns without fear of retribution.

3. **Encourage Repentance**: Create an environment where repentance is encouraged and facilitated. This involves providing support for those who seek to change their behaviors and offering forgiveness and guidance.

4. **Emphasize Empathy and Love**: Teach and model the importance of empathy and genuine love for one another. Encourage congregants to build strong, supportive relationships based on mutual respect and care.

5. **Focus on Servant Leadership**: Promote the principles of servant leadership, where leaders prioritize the needs of their congregants and seek to serve rather than be served. This aligns with the biblical model of leadership exemplified by Jesus Christ.

By learning from the mistakes and redemptive journeys of biblical figures, the church can take proactive steps to address narcissism and foster a healthy, Christ-centered community. Through humility, accountability, and a focus on servanthood, the church can effectively counter the detrimental effects of narcissistic behavior and build a strong, united body of believers. Narcissism poses a significant challenge to relationships and leadership within the Christian sector and church walls. Its effects can be deeply damaging, leading to a breakdown in trust, spiritual harm, and inhibited growth. However, the Bible offers clear guidance on humility, love, empathy, integrity, and accountability, providing a blueprint for overcoming narcissistic tendencies.

Addressing narcissism requires a concerted effort from individuals, leaders, and the broader church community. Through personal reflection, communal support, and systemic changes, the church can foster an environment where humility, servanthood, and genuine love for one another prevail. By doing so, the church can more effectively fulfill its mission of shepherding believers and spreading the message of Christ's love and grace.

Religious Spirits vs. The Holy Spirit

By Ashley Thompson

"To fall in love with God is the greatest romance, to seek him the greatest adventure, to find him, the greatest human achievement."

—St. Augustine of Hippo

The Lord gave me another message. He said, "Go and shout this message to Jerusalem. This is what the Lord says: "I remember how eager you were to please me as a young bride long ago, how you loved me and followed me even through the barren wilderness... This is what the Lord *says: "What did your ancestors find wrong with me that led them to stray so far from me? They worshiped worthless idols only to become worthless themselves.*

—*Jeremiah 2:1-2, 5 NLT*

The Bride of Christ is the most precious, beautiful, and valuable treasure Jesus owns. His church is His bride. To touch the natural wife of a king evokes severe punishment, for her stature is elevated by the love of her king.

She is guarded by the power and authority of her kingly husband. If men throughout history were punished because they touched a king's spouse, can you imagine the consequences of those who willfully harm, defile, or seduce the Beloved of Christ? To touch the bride of the King of kings and Lord of lords, the Ruler of heaven and earth, is infinitely more *dangerous*. For our King is eternally devoted and sacrificially given over to His bride. You are a part of the precious Bride of Christ.

This great and mighty King acts justly and has a heart perfumed with sweet mercy. This glorious King is, *"chief among ten thousand"* (Song of Solomon 5:10 NKJV). He is perfect in beauty, grace, wisdom, power, and holiness. He walks on a street of *"pure gold, like transparent glass"* and His gates are *"made of a single pearl"* (Revelation 21:21 ESV). He is worshiped and adored by majestic angels and creation heralds His praises. He is incomparable and everything the bride could ever want. As omnipotent as He is, He doesn't force Himself on His Beloved even though He created her for Himself. He has given her one of the loftiest gifts—free will. He asks His Bride to respond to His call for a covenantal relationship and leaves it up to her to say "yes." He has everything prepared, everything she needs *"for life and godliness"* (2 Peter 1:3 TPT) He loves His Bride with an undying, selflessness that is wholehearted. But this King has an enemy His Bride is unfamiliar with.

Now, picture a husband on his wedding day, dressed up in finery, as he watches the aisle anxiously to see his lover. I've seen husbands so overcome at weddings that they cry or almost jolt back in surprise when they see their beautiful bride. Some men jump with joy or break out into a spontaneous little dance. There's always a special kind of smile on their faces, a smile reserved only for their future wife. Now, what would you suppose would happen if some murderer came running down the aisle grabbed the bride's arm, and attempted to drag her away? I bet the groom would start swinging his fists, giving that criminal a good beating until he released her. I imagine Jesus has more protective instincts for His Bride than a natural husband who would readily defend his fiancé. Unfortunately, the enemy of the Bride of Christ is a lot cleverer than that. He doesn't often use physical force.

This pretentious swindler has one goal, and that's to steal from Jesus's Bride, destroy everything good in her life (including her relationship with the One who loves her most) and kill her. It's the only way he knows how to hurt the holy Bridegroom.

This villain is running rampant on Earth today using an excellent reconnaissance strategy. He has studied humanity since its inception. He knows humans were originally created with a spirit that was made for connection with the God Head (Father, Son, and Holy Spirit) but we were separated from our core relationship through the sin he inspired— which has left mankind thirsty for spiritual life. So, he maliciously disguises himself as Christ, the only One who can satisfy our thirst and connect us again to God. The enemy knows without this unity, we can't be whole. We are hopelessly incomplete without Jesus.

> *For such men are false apostles [spurious, counterfeits], deceitful workmen, masquerading as apostles (special messengers) of Christ (the Messiah). And it is no wonder, for Satan himself masquerades as an angel of light; So it is not surprising if his servants also masquerade as ministers of righteousness. [But] their end will correspond with their deeds.*
> —2 Corinthians 11:13-15 AMPC

He has many evil demon minions who do his dark bidding through knowing or unknowing humans. This crook has made his way through countless churches and stolen the Bride of Christ from her Bridegroom in the most surreptitious way. He comes disguised as her *Groom*. He has known her Groom for thousands of years longer than she has. He can quote the Bridegroom's words with such minute subtleties that unless the Bride knows her groom closely, she can be fooled by him. Imagine how Jesus must feel when His prized Bride is seduced, deceived, and then *harmed* by an imposter who claims to be the King she loves.

Lucifer has envied the Father, Son, and Holy Spirit for eons. He has tried his best shot to usurp God and be like the Most High…but he failed miserably (see Isaiah 14: 13-15).

However, he appears to be consumed with jealousy for he has not stopped trying to be like Jesus (antichrist). One of his favorite cloaks is religion. He often uses religious spirits to leaven the faith of countless believers. He loves to pervert scripture with a forked tongue. He has been corrupting the Word of God in the consciences of men since the garden where he beguiled Eve. And he's been slowly choking the Bride with suffocating dead works, legalism, condemnation, and an assortment of other traps in his cache. He kills slowly like a python, constricting the air of the Holy Spirit's influence in the Bride through wrong doctrines.

The religious spirit has abused the Bride and made her believe that the inflicted pain was from God (Father, Son, and Holy Spirit). He has criminalized the reputation of God in her heart. He has acted like a masterful prosecutor as he defames Christ and the believer he's influencing. His accusations are calculated. He has successfully smoldered the fire of first love that once burned brightly in her heart. He has left her inner soul a wasteland of bitterness, unforgiveness, shame, anger, guilt and loaded her down with unbearable burdens. For years, I was befuddled by a heart-killing religious spirit who was effectively separating my soul from Jesus.

Jesus used many things to reveal to me the truth, and I finally came to see that I was lost in religion (a room of smoke and mirrors). I had a dream about this. Before I share the dream, please know, I don't want to paint the gothic churches in Europe as evil. Also, it is not my intent to come against the Catholic church, nor to say that all Catholics are being influenced by a religious spirit. I am simply sharing my dream. I know many beautiful born-again saints from different denominations. I believe religious spirits are in many denominations and "houses of worship." The enemy doesn't discriminate. He isn't biased. His targeting landing points are in the individual hearts of man, not certain church affiliations. We don't battle against flesh and blood and the Body of Christ certainly should never discriminate against each other. We are to walk in love and in the unity that comes from obedience to the Lordship of Jesus.

In my dream, I was in a towering Gothic cathedral. This massive church was charcoal black with accents of hellish red. It was tall like a skyscraper, and it reminded me of the castle-like churches in Germany. I was inside of this church and couldn't find my way out. The inside of it was like a haunted mansion: cold, dark, and eerie with an ominous presence. There were so many rooms, creepy wall hangings, and artifacts. I was not only lost, but I was running from a demon that took the form of a predatory spiritual T-Rex who was seeking to marry me. (I know it sounds crazy.)

I managed to escape him, and I slipped, opening a secret room by accidentally setting off a disguised lever. I crawled inside and the space opened to another large room. I instinctively knew I shouldn't be in this room because it was meant for those in church governance. Before me was a large spiral staircase and behind me was a small, dank alcove. Some people were coming down the stairs, so I crouched into the tiny nook and hid. I saw the shadows of the three people before I could see them. The way the light was in the room elongated their shadows.

I looked intently and finally, two "priests" appeared, and sandwiched between them was the "pope." They were dressed in elaborate religious frocks. As they ceremoniously descended the stairs, their shadows flickered on the wall like a dying lightbulb. Each time this happened, I saw a different shape appear. It was unlike their physical forms. As the shadows flickered,

I saw the spirits that were within them, and it made my spine cold and my body shiver. To my horror, the two priests' shadows revealed demons. The "pope's" shadow exposed the antichrist spirit. I cried out in anguish! These were the "clergy" millions of people depended on to show them the way to God. They were not leading them to God. They were separating them from a life-transforming relationship with Jesus and were leading them into spiritual darkness.

The realization of this grieved me and I hit the floor in deep sorrow. I travailed loudly in tongues and curled up into a fetal position. Suddenly, the antichrist spirit in the "pope" picked up on the presence of the Holy Spirit like a honing device. He teleported to where I was. His skin was wrinkled, gaunt, and gray. I had never seen a more ill-looking "man." He was the closest thing to a living zombie I have ever seen in a dream. His eyes were like black holes, and he began forcefully digging his fingers into his face and pulling on his cheeks until his skin looked like it would rip off. The spirit within him was furious, but it couldn't touch me. I knew it wasn't angry with me; it was angry at the *presence* of *the Holy Spirit*! He started screaming at me, "Shut up! Shut up! SHUT UUUUPPPPPPPPP!" I kept on crying out in tongues. Suddenly I woke up from my dream, feeling chilled.

> *For I am jealous for you with the jealousy of God himself. I promised you as a pure bride to one husband—Christ. But I fear that somehow your pure and undivided devotion to Christ will be corrupted, just as Eve was deceived by the cunning ways of the serpent. You happily put up with whatever anyone tells you, even if they preach a different Jesus than the one we preach, or a different kind of Spirit than the one you received, or a different kind of gospel than the one you believed.*
> —*2 Corinthians 11:2-4 NLT*

The religious spirit operates in churches across the world. It relentlessly seeks to discourage and quench the presence of the Holy Spirit in believers.

It raises a critical eye on the operation of the gifts of the Holy Spirit in church. Some believers have been told that the gifts were just for the early apostles. This nefarious spirit also works against the fruit of the Holy Spirit by discouraging the Christian *from the simple faith it takes to consider himself* "dead to sin" and "alive to God in Christ Jesus" (see Romans 6:11, NIV). There is a very *important* reason for this. Jesus was filled with the Holy Spirit (see John 3:34). Jesus was led by the Holy Spirit (see Luke 4:1). Jesus didn't enter ministry until after the Holy Spirit came upon Him as a dove at His baptism (see Luke 3:23 NLT). He performed no miracles until the Holy Spirit was with Him (see Luke 4). In fact, Jesus' first sermon highlights the Holy Spirit's significance when it came to Him accomplishing *everything* God sent Him to do:

> *"The Spirit of the* LORD *is upon me for he has anointed me to bring Good News to the poor. He has sent me to proclaim that captives will be released, that the blind will see, that the oppressed will be set free, and that the time of the* LORD's *favor has come."*
>
> —Luke 4:18 NLT

Jesus is our example. We are to follow Him. If Jesus walked with the Holy Spirit, I firmly believe we should too. In fact, before Jesus ascended, He commanded His disciples to wait until they received the Holy Spirit: *"And now I will send the Holy Spirit, just as my Father promised. But stay here in the city until the Holy Spirit comes and fills you with power from heaven"* (Luke 24:49 NLT).

> Jesus explained to His followers that they would be a witness to the world through the Holy Spirit. *"But you will receive power and ability when the Holy Spirit comes upon you; and you will be My witnesses [to tell people about Me] both in Jerusalem and in all Judea, and Samaria, and even to the ends of the earth"* (Acts 1:8 AMP). Jesus declared a

special honor on the Holy Spirit when He said, *"Therefore I say to you, every sin and blasphemy will be forgiven men, but the blasphemy against the Spirit will not be forgiven men. Anyone who speaks a word against the Son of Man, it will be forgiven him; but whoever speaks against the Holy Spirit, it will not be forgiven him, either in this age or in the age to come"* (Matthew 12:31-32 NKJV). Imagine that. People can be forgiven for blaspheming *Jesus*, but they cannot be forgiven for blaspheming the *Holy Spirit*. If Jesus placed this much importance on the Holy Spirit, we should too.

Without the Holy Spirit, the effectiveness and quality of life of the Christian is greatly diminished. I would even venture to say, it is *impossible* to live a victorious life without Him. Yet, He is unwelcomed or looked upon with suspicion in many churches.

Let's look at how religious spirits were operating against the movement of the Holy Spirit in Jesus' day and how it compares with today. There's nothing new under the sun (see Ecclesiastes 1:9).

In Matthew 9:33, Jesus cast a demon out of someone who was mute. Once the demon was driven out, the man was able to speak. Instead of rejoicing at this man's new freedom, the Pharisees charged the glorious work of the Holy Spirit to the work of the prince of demons. (see Matthew 9:34). This is *blasphemous*.

This spirit perpetuates teachings that infiltrate the purity of faith in the consciences of people. Jesus called certain doctrinal teachings "leaven." In Matthew 16:6, He warned His disciples to watch out for the leaven of the Pharisees and Sadducees. Then they understood how he cautioned them not to beware of the leaven of bread, but of the doctrine of the Pharisees and the Sadducees (see Matthew 16:12 KJV). Interestingly, this leaven was coming from the leaders of the synagogue (church). These religious leaders were ultimately the ones responsible for the wrongful prosecution of Jesus. They almost caused a riot to pressure Pilot into allowing the crucifixion of Jesus (see Matthew 27:20 NLT). In our modern world, it would be like a group of influential Christian leaders gathering to execute Jesus.

To bake a loaf of bread, you need just a little bit of yeast (leaven) to cause the whole batch to rise. A sprinkle is all it takes and once the leaven is mixed in, it spreads to every part of the dough. This is how false teachings work. A little alteration of the truth is potent enough to infect *every* area of someone's belief system. This leaven keeps the kingdom of God from being fruitful in the believer's life.

> *"But woe (judgment is coming) to you, [self-righteous] scribes and Pharisees, hypocrites, because you shut off the kingdom of heaven in front of people; for you do not enter yourselves, nor do you allow those who are [in the process of] entering to do so... Woe to you, [self-righteous] scribes and Pharisees, hypocrites, because you travel over sea and land to make a single proselyte (convert to Judaism), and when he becomes a convert, you make him twice as much a son of hell as you are."*
> —Matthew 23:13, 15 AMP

Stephen, the first church martyr recorded in scripture, spoke about the opposition toward the Holy Spirit in Acts 7:51-52 (NIV), *"You stiff-necked people! Your hearts and ears are still uncircumcised. You are just like your ancestors. You always resist the Holy Spirit. Was there ever a prophet your ancestors did not persecute? They even killed those who predicted the coming of the Righteous One. And now you have betrayed and murdered him."* Religious spirits have been in operation for thousands of years coaxing people to resist the Holy Spirit and the Anointed One (a name for Jesus representing the fact that he was anointed with the Holy Spirit). A study of the nation of Israel, the Dark

Ages in Europe, and even modern Christianity will show the evidence of this demonic presence.

Years ago, I was being plagued so cruelly by religious spirits that I thought I had lost my salvation and that I was going to hell. The burden of guilt weighed heavily on me. God used a man from my church, who was full of grace and the Holy Spirit, to bring about an area of healing in my life. Interestingly, this man was discouraged by church policy from meeting with me because I was a single woman, and he was married. I can understand the reasons and natural wisdom for a "rule" like this. For a while, I refused to reach out to Steve about my torment because of this code of ethics. One day as I was being tormented, I cried out to God, and I felt like I should call Steve. I didn't have his number, so I walked to the church secretary's office and after exchanging small talk, I politely asked for it. I masked the pain and turmoil I was suffering inside. The secretary was a homely, sweet lady and she had known me since I was a little girl. I was very involved with my church through volunteer work and youth leadership so I'm assuming she thought nothing of my request (thankfully).

She looked up his number and gave it to me. Before long, I left. Once out of earshot, I hurriedly called Steve and asked him to please come pray with me now. Steve briefly spoke with his wife and once she gave her consent, he told me on the phone, "Your torment will end today. I am coming and the Lord Jesus will touch you and you will be well." I felt the power in his words, and I even felt the spirits who were tormenting me react inside of my body. "Okay," I quivered, struggling to hold in my tears.

I chose a blue chair in the corner of the church to sit down as I waited for Steve. Thankfully, no one was inside the building at this time. I thank God that nobody was there because I don't know if they would have interfered or if I wouldn't have felt comfortable enough to tell Steve what was going on had someone else been there. I was so religious at this time that I almost always wore a mask at church. I worked to keep on a fake mask of perfection.

Steve entered, dressed casually, and sat down beside me. There was something about him that made me comfortable and feel free enough to share my deepest and darkest secrets. As I shared, I began to cry. Tears of shame and self-blame trailed down my cheeks. Steve patiently waited until I was done. I noticed he never reacted in disgust or condemnation toward the things I had confessed to him. Afterward, he began to preach the gospel to me. "Ashley, God paid for your sins over two thousand years ago when Jesus took your place on the cross. The judgment of God is swallowed up on the cross for those who believe in Christ."

I began to slowly wipe away my tears as he spoke. His rich brown eyes gazed at me like I was a woman of worth. He went even further. "You are the righteousness of God in Christ. You are a beloved daughter of God Almighty. Your past is forgotten under the blood of Jesus. You don't need to look back at what you've done. God sees you as holy and pure through his Son. Look at Jesus." He then began to explain how this was typified in the Old Testament when the Israelites would bring an animal to be a burnt sacrifice for their sins. "The priest never looked at the Israelites to see if they were perfect. He knew they weren't. Otherwise, they wouldn't need to bring a sacrifice. Instead, the priest examined the animal to see if it was perfect according to God's law as a worthy sacrifice. The Israelites never had to worry so long as their sacrifice was perfect. Ashley, God is *not looking at you* to see if you've measured up to earn his deliverance or love. *He's looking at Jesus,* your perfect sacrifice. He's checking out his holy Son and as long as Jesus is perfect, then you don't have to fret. You don't have to keep trying to work to earn anything from God that He's provided through His Son."

The more Steve talked, the more I felt the invisible presence of the Holy Spirit tangibly. I began to feel hope again and believe that I *could* be free. It was like witnessing a glorious sunrise after months of darkness. His words were palpable with power and inside of me, I felt the unclean spirits moving rapidly. I felt an evil spirit move from my belly area to my head, as if to block the truth I was hearing. I responsively placed my hand against the pressure and mumbled, "I have a headache."

Steve's eyes quickened and he stood before leaning a little toward me. He spoke softly, "Release my sister." I knew he was talking directly to the demonic spirit trying to hinder and resist the work of the Holy Spirit in my life. He began to breathe on me. As he breathed, the physical presence of the Holy Spirit through his breath came over me. It was *amazing*! Suddenly, the demon fled in a fury and hit Steve as it escaped. Steve jerked back and now his eyes were large. "Something was trying to hinder you," he said.

"And the believers were filled with joy and with the Holy Spirit."
—Acts 15:32 NLT

For the first time in years, I felt the glory of the gospel. A heavenly bliss expanded in me that was beautiful. I began to laugh, quietly at first, and then explosively. Steve began laughing with me. Soon, our laughter was floating up to the church's ceiling and reverberating off the walls like bells of freedom. I began to rejoice with joy unspeakable…full of glory (see 1 Peter 1:8). I don't remember how long I laughed, but it was a wonderful experience. Hearing the gospel preached through the power of the Holy Spirit is *liberating*! Shortly after that encounter, I went off to Bible college and saw God perform many miracles in my life. The mighty power of the gospel became a reality for me as I dwelt on the grace of God, continually sifting out religious leaven and relying on the finished work of Jesus.

I remember a woman at Bible college telling me how she hadn't had an appetite for three years because of surgery on her stomach that went wrong. I didn't bat an eye. I was so focused on Jesus (thus not being focused or reliant on myself) that I asked her, "Do you want Jesus to heal you of that?"

She responded slightly with doubt, "I've had it for so long."

Her doubt washed over me like water off a duck's back. Undeterred, I asked her again, "Do you want Jesus to heal you of that?"

She nodded. I gently placed my hand on her arm and said a simple prayer. "Jesus, thank You for paying for my sister's healing. Touch her body and correct whatever is wrong."

About two days later, she found me, as if she had been searching for me, and she exclaimed, "You'll never guess what?! My appetite is back!"

I gave a soft smile, probably lacking the enthusiastic response she was expecting. "That's good. Praise Jesus."

She stood there dumbfounded for a few seconds. I sort of turned my attention back to the stage where the teacher was scheduled to be any minute. I could see her still standing there from my peripheral vision. She left quietly, moments later. Looking back, I didn't respond with much hype because things like that were becoming common in my experience. Once I hugged a roommate, and she felt the presence of the Holy Spirit touch her.

Her eyes gleamed and she said, "Something went into me from you." Steve had prophesied over me months before that the Lord told him that people would begin to feel the Holy Spirit sometimes when I hugged them.

Years later, this still happens.

I sometimes picture religion as a glass of ocean water given to a thirsty man. If a person was severely dehydrated, drinking salty water would kill them faster. It would do more damage than good. Religion is like this. There are people in the world who are thirsty for God. They come to churches, they talk to Christians, and they leave thirstier than when they came.

I'd like to share my own quote based on my experiences: "Religion is like giving a cup of salty ocean water to a man dying of thirst. It kills its victims faster than if they had no water at all. Relationship with God through the Holy Spirit is fresh, living water. He is the vital gift from God that every believer needs to live an abundant life."

Jesus promised that those who drink from the water He gives will thirst no more (see John 4:14). He specifically says, *"The water I give will become a spring of water gushing up inside that person, giving eternal life"* (John 4:14 NCV).

As a child of God, this promise is for *you*. You were never meant to go through life in your own strength. You are meant to receive your source of life from God Himself. God loved you so much that He gave His one and only Son so that you might believe and be saved. He didn't end His goodness there…He also poured out His very Spirit! You are meant to abide in Christ and walk in the Spirit according to the Word. You are meant to experience the power of the Holy Spirit here and now.

I pray God uses this chapter to encourage you to walk in the anointing of His Spirit. I pray He uses this to inspire you to live in the fullness of your inheritance in Christ.

> *He has qualified us [making us sufficient] as ministers of a new covenant [of salvation through Christ], not of the letter [of a written code] but of the Spirit; for the letter [of the Law] kills [by revealing sin and demanding obedience], but the Spirit gives life.*
>
> —*2 Corinthians 3:6 AMP*

About Author Ashley Thompson

"Ashley Thompson is a blessed daughter of God, wife, and mother, whose passion is to see people enter a deep, personal relationship with Jesus Christ. She loves spending quality time with her heavenly Father and has authored books from those sacred moments (*Visions of Celestial Love* and *Romantic Rendezvous for the Soul*). In 2023 she published her first children's story book, *Fallen Coins*.

She holds a B.A. in Biblical studies from Charis Bible college and two A.A's with honors in English and Humanities. Ashley is a certified Life Breakthrough coach and is certified in New Testament Leadership from

Impact International School of Ministry. She worked as a prayer minister for AWMI and has prayed for thousands of people. She is thankful for every miracle she's seen through the work of the Holy Spirit.

Ashley was born on the tropical island of Nassau Bahamas but grew up on a cool Mediterranean coast in California. She has over ten years of experience in various human services. She currently works for Set Free Monterey Bay, a wonderful Christian organization that cares for women who have escaped human trafficking. She is an effervescent worship dancer and often uses her streamer and flags to express her adoration to God.

Her love language is words of affirmation, and she savors heart-to-heart conversations where there is mutual vulnerability, depth of soul, and prayerful openness to the Spirit of God. She believes in the healing power of God to mend the body as well as the heart and mind. Since 2022, she has taught Bible classes at a private Christian school. She loves scented candles, flowy dresses, vibrant flowers, big glitter earrings, chai lattes, Christmas lights, the deep, azure water of the Pacific Ocean, and chocolate. Her passion is Jesus and those He loves! To learn more about Ashley visit: www.NourishmentThroughWords.com

PART II
Testimony Chapters

From the Depths of Betrayal to the Heights of Triumph

By Dr. Sherley Lefevre

(All scriptures were taken from the New International Version of the Bible)

The church, a sanctuary for many, had become the crucible of my trials. Each pew, each hymnal, and each stained-glass window held memories of the hurt I had endured. For years, I had been the underdog, the one without pedigree and shunned and overlooked. Yet, like Joseph, who was betrayed by his brothers but rose to greatness, I found my way through the darkness into a place of light and victory. The echoes of whispered doubts and the weight of judgmental gazes had shaped me into a resilient soul, tempered by adversity yet steadfast in faith. Amidst the solemn silence of prayers, I discovered not only solace but also a profound sense of purpose; a calling to uplift others burdened by similar trials, to be a beacon of hope amidst the shadows.

The Abuse from Men of Power

The worst sting came from those who held positions of power—men who were supposed to shepherd the flock but instead preyed upon the vulnerable.

Their words, laced with manipulation and deceit, were like arrows that pierced my soul. They used their sermons to disguise their true intentions, wielding scripture like a weapon rather than a balm.

There were three so-called "men of God", in particular, who marked my journey with profound pain. They were all from different churches at various points in my life. These men comprised the only significant relationships I ever had, and each one left a scar that ran deep into the core of my soul. The most recent offender who was supposed to be my soulmate was a preacher who, behind his charismatic façade, harbored a darkness that slowly revealed itself. He spoke of love and charity from the pulpit, but his actions at home were far from loving. He isolated me from friends and family, ensuring I was entirely dependent on him. His financial control was suffocating; he monitored every penny I spent, making sure I knew my place was beneath him. His emotional abuse was relentless, tearing down my self-worth piece by piece. He twisted scripture to justify his control, saying, "Wives, submit yourselves to your own husbands as you do to the Lord" (Ephesians 5:22), ignoring the mutual respect and love that the passage calls for. As time passed, the abuse escalated beyond emotional wounds, manifesting in physical threats that left me fearing for my safety and ultimately forced me to make the agonizing decision to leave the marriage.

The second man was a Pastor who initially seemed like a safe haven of support about 11 years ago. He offered a shoulder to cry on and words of comfort when I was at my lowest. But soon, his true nature emerged. He used my vulnerabilities to exploit me, demanding more and more while giving nothing in return. His emotional abuse turned physical; each strike was accompanied by a twisted interpretation of scripture meant to break my spirit further. His hands, meant to bless, were heavy with condemnation and abuse. His abuse escalated to terrifying levels, especially as we approached engagement. One day, in a fit of rage, he choked me almost to death. His hands were around my neck, cutting off my breath, and leaving me with the thought I was going to die. When he released his grip, it was only to punch me repeatedly, his fists colliding with my body like hammers. Before this moment, he threw me into a glass mirror, which miraculously did not leave physical scars but indelibly left emotional scars. His verbal abuse was a constant barrage, belittling me, telling me I was worthless, and that no one would ever believe me if I spoke out.

My son's father was the third and the least recent among them, which occurred over a decade ago. He was a man who was seemingly on fire for God and a powerful preacher when we fell in love and decided to get married almost 20 years ago. However, I look back now and realize that he preyed on my need for belonging and acceptance. He showered me with attention and promises of a bright future, only to withdraw his affection shortly after we were married, abandon my son and me when he was only 5 years old and left us to suffer a great deal of hardship and humiliation. Not only did he abandon me to raise my son alone, but he also served me divorce papers without any logical explanation months after his departure. My heart and soul were crushed, to say the least. His manipulations left me in a constant state of anxiety, always striving to be what he wanted, yet never feeling good enough. During the course of our relationship, He wielded emotional abuse like a finely honed instrument, using praise to draw me in and then cruelly withdrawing it to punish me. Each act of kindness was a prelude to manipulation; he would build me up just to tear me down, leaving me doubting my worth and sanity. The emotional rollercoaster was exhausting, with highs of fleeting approval followed by crushing lows of disapproval and disdain. His sudden departure was a final, devastating blow, reinforcing the lie that I was unworthy of love and support, leaving me to pick up the pieces of my shattered self-esteem and faith.

"Beware of false prophets, who come to you in sheep's clothing, but inwardly are ravenous wolves" (Matthew 7:15). This verse echoed in my mind as I recalled the way all of these men twisted holy words to justify their actions. Eventually, each encounter with them deepened my wounds, turning what should have been seasons of joyful harvesting into remorse and torment.

Their hands and mouths, meant to heal and bless, became instruments of pain, locking me in a cage of fear filled with uncertainties about my future, my calling, and my destiny.

Through their actions, these men distorted the very essence of faith, using it as a tool for their gain. But even in the darkest moments, I clung to the hope that the true nature of God was not reflected in their actions. It was this hope that kept me going, that fueled my determination to rise above the abuse and reclaim my life. And as I look back, I see not just the pain, but the strength I gained from enduring it. Today I can lead a women's ministry and lovingly counsel women from all over the globe who are facing difficulties in their relationships, self-esteem, identifying their purpose and calling, or healing from past traumas. I owe all of this to the trials that I endured with these men in my life. What the devil meant to destroy me, God certainly turned it around and used it for my good. He placed a love and a passion in me to serve others both locally and abroad. My current position as a global humanitarian stems directly from the emotional, psychological, physical, and spiritual wounds inflicted upon me. God allowed me to be wounded so that I can be a vessel to help others heal.

The Fake Friends and Jealous Hearts

Then there were the friends who were *anything but*. They wore masks of piety and kindness, but behind closed doors, their envy festered. They whispered behind my back, their words like venom spreading through the congregation. I was an easy target, an outsider who didn't fit their mold of perfection. I trusted them implicitly, sharing my hopes, dreams, and fears, believing in their friendship and support. We prayed together, broke bread together, and I confided in them during my darkest moments, expecting them to stand by me as true friends would.

"Even my close friend, someone I trusted, one who shared my bread, has turned against me" (Psalm 41:9). The betrayal of those I considered friends cut deep. Their jealousy was palpable, their smiles never reaching their eyes. They seemed to relish in my struggles, taking pleasure in seeing me falter. When I needed them the most, during the tumultuous times of abuse and despair, they were nowhere to be found. Their absence was deafening, a stark contrast to their previous declarations of loyalty and support. Instead of standing by me, they distanced themselves, more concerned with maintaining their facades than offering me a helping hand.

Their betrayal was a double-edged sword. Not only did they fail to support me, but they also turned others against me, spreading malicious rumors and falsehoods. It felt like being attacked from all sides, with no safe place to turn. Their gossip and slander isolated me further, amplifying my pain and loneliness. Each time I saw them at church, their friendly greetings and false concerns were salt in the wounds, a reminder of their deceit and my misplaced trust.

In my moments of greatest need, their betrayal was a stark reminder of human fallibility and the superficiality that can hide behind a façade of piety. It was a painful lesson in discernment and the importance of seeking out genuine, compassionate connections. Yet, through this profound hurt, I also learned to lean more heavily on God, finding solace in His unwavering presence when human companionship failed me. Despite the challenges I faced, I continued to persevere, and I continued to attend church since my faith was rooted in God and not people or their treatment of me.

Ostracized for My Lack of Pedigree

In a world where lineage and social standing meant everything, my lack of pedigree was a mark against me in my Christian circle I was constantly reminded of my place, or rather, my lack thereof. The elite circles closed ranks, leaving me on the outside looking in. It was a harsh reality, to be judged not for who I was, but for where I came from. I was not born into a Christian family. I began to go to church as a teen and converted to Christianity at the age of 15.

This lack of a Christian upbringing was a constant shadow, a reminder to others of my "inferior" status. Many of my friends had grown up steeped in church traditions, their families embedded in the fabric of the congregation for generations. Their knowledge of scripture and church etiquette seemed second nature, while I was learning anew, with each step feeling scrutinized and judged. Despite my fervent faith and genuine commitment, I was viewed as an outsider, an intruder in their tight-knit community.

The whispers behind my back often echoed this sentiment. "She's not one of us," is what their attitudes and behaviors towards me would scream laced with an undertone of superiority. My lack of a Christian lineage was a convenient tool for them to question my faith, my motives, and my place among them. Even my sincere efforts to contribute and belong were met with skepticism. My ideas and opinions were often dismissed, not on their merit, but because of my background. It was a constant uphill battle to prove myself, to show that my faith was just as real and profound as theirs, despite my different starting point. By the grace of God, I occupied over the years many roles that spanned from Sunday School teacher, Praise Dance instructor, Choir director, Youth Vice President and Women's Ministry leader. Yet none of these occupied roles or my abundance of gifts and skillset proved to be enough to give me access to the "inner circle."

This exclusion was most painful during moments that should have been joyous. Celebrations, community gatherings, and social events became reminders of my outsider status. Invitations that never came, conversations that abruptly ended when I approached, and the subtle yet unmistakable signals of exclusion all took their toll. It was as if my lack of pedigree was a stain that could not be washed away, a permanent mark of "otherness."

"Do not judge by appearances, but judge with right judgment" (John 7:24). Yet, judgment came swiftly and harshly. My contributions were dismissed, and my voice silenced. I was made to feel unworthy, an outcast in a place that preached love and acceptance. But through it all, I found solace in my faith and the knowledge that God looked at my heart, not my history. In His eyes, I was not an outsider but a beloved child, deserving of love and grace. This truth sustained me, giving me the strength to persevere and rise above prejudice and exclusion, forging my path not based on human approval but on divine acceptance and love.

Rising Above: The Underdog's Triumph

But God had a different plan. Just as David, the shepherd boy, was chosen to be king despite being overlooked by his own family, I found strength in my faith. "But the Lord said to Samuel, 'Do not consider his appearance or his height, for I have rejected him. The Lord does not look at the things people look at. People look at the outward appearance, but the Lord looks at the heart'" (1 Samuel 16:7).

I began to focus on the love and grace of God, rather than the condemnation of others. With each slight, I grew stronger and more determined. I found solace in prayer, and comfort in the scriptures. The more they tried to push me down, the higher I rose. I connected with others who had been ostracized. Among them were those who stayed and those who left the church, building a community of support and love.

In those quiet moments of prayer, I felt God's presence more profoundly than ever. It was as if He was whispering to my heart, reminding me of my worth and His unconditional love. "For I know the plans I have for you," declares the Lord, "plans to prosper you and not to harm you, plans to give you hope and a future" (Jeremiah 29:11). These words became a lifeline, a promise that my suffering was not in vain and that He had a greater purpose for my life.

I immersed myself in the Bible, drawing strength from stories of perseverance and divine justice. I found inspiration in the perseverance of Job, the faith of Abraham, and the courage of Esther. Each story reinforced the truth that God uses the seemingly insignificant and overlooked to accomplish His grand purposes. My faith became my armor, shielding me from the barbs of judgment and rejection.

As I delved deeper into my faith, I discovered a resilience I didn't know I possessed. I began to see my trials not as burdens, but as opportunities for growth and testimony. I realized that my journey could inspire others who were struggling, showing them that God's grace is sufficient even in the darkest of times. "My grace is sufficient for you, for my power is made perfect in weakness" (2 Corinthians 12:9). This verse resonated deeply with me, a reminder that in my weakness, God's strength was most evident.

I also found kindred spirits, individuals who had faced similar rejections and hurts. Together, we formed a community bound by shared experiences and a collective hope in God's redemptive power. We supported each other, prayed together, and shared our stories, creating a space where everyone was valued and loved. This community became a source of immense strength, proving that even in our brokenness, we could find healing and purpose.

Through this journey, I learned to forgive those who had wronged me. "And be kind and compassionate to one another, forgiving each other, just as in Christ God forgave you" (Ephesians 4:32). Forgiveness was not easy, but it was necessary for my healing. By releasing the bitterness and resentment, I freed myself from the chains of the past, allowing God's love to fill the spaces where hurt once resided.

In time, my resilience and faith were recognized. Opportunities opened up, and I found myself in positions of influence and respect. The very people who had once looked down on me now sought my counsel. I had come full circle, from the depths of betrayal to the heights of triumph. For reasons I can't explain, God restored me like Joseph and caused the same hands that rejected me to be extended towards me for assistance, empowerment, inspiration and revelation. I can't tell you at what point of my journey things began to turn around, but I just know that God turned it. I was able to go back in love and serve my former church members via preaching, sharing my testimony, hosting a conference and so much more over the years. My journey was a testament to the transformative power of God's love and grace, a living proof that with faith, perseverance, and forgiveness, one can rise above the ashes and soar.

A Testament to Faith and Resilience

This chapter of my life is a testament to the strength found in faith and resilience. It is a reminder that no matter how deep the hurt, there is always hope for healing and redemption. The church, once a place of pain, has become a place of triumph. My story is not just one of survival, but of overcoming and thriving. And for that, I am eternally grateful.

Through the crucible of suffering, I discovered a wellspring of inner strength and an unshakeable faith in God's goodness. Each trial and tribulation refined me, stripping away the superficial and revealing the core of who I am: a beloved child of God, resilient and empowered. The wounds inflicted by others, though deep and painful, became the scars that now mark my journey of healing and growth.

My story is also a source of inspiration for others who walk a similar path. It is a testament to the power of God's grace to transform even the most painful experiences into sources of strength and inspiration. "And we know that in all things God works for the good of those who love him, who have been called according to his purpose" (Romans 8:28). This promise holds true in my life, as the very trials that sought to break me became the foundation of my testimony.

The relationships I have now are built on authenticity and mutual respect, grounded in the love of Christ. The community of support and love that I have found is a stark contrast to the isolation and betrayal of the past.

These relationships are a testament to the healing power of genuine, Christ-centered fellowship.

In reflecting on my journey, I see God's hand in every step. From the moments of despair to the heights of triumph, He has been my constant companion, guiding me, strengthening me, and ultimately lifting me to a place of peace and purpose. "The Lord is close to the brokenhearted and saves those who are crushed in spirit" (Psalm 34:18). This truth has been evident in my life, as each heartbreak was met with divine comfort and each defeat with divine victory.

As I look to the future, I am filled with hope and anticipation. I know that the same God who brought me through the darkness will continue to lead me into the light. My past no longer holds power over me; it is a testament to God's redemptive power and a source of strength as I move forward. With faith as my foundation and resilience as my guide, I am ready to embrace all that God has in store, knowing that I am never alone and that my story is far from over.

This journey, while filled with ups and downs, thistles and thorns has blessed me immensely. I have learned how to love like Christ, serve like Christ and suffer like Christ.

In closing, I invite you to join me in embracing the transformative power of faith and resilience. Let my story serve as a reminder for those who are walking through their own valleys of pain and betrayal. May you find the courage to confront your own struggles, knowing that you are not alone, and that God's love and grace are sufficient to carry you through.

Let us remember that no matter how deep the hurt, there is always hope for healing and redemption. Together, let us reclaim the sanctity of our churches, turning them from places of pain into arenas of triumph. Let us cultivate communities of genuine love and acceptance, where all are valued and embraced for who they are.

May we each commit to being agents of change, standing against abuse and injustice wherever we encounter it. Let us extend a hand of compassion and support to those who have been wounded, offering them the hope and healing that comes from knowing Christ.

This is our call to action: to rise above our past, to stand firm in our faith, and to embrace the abundant life that God has promised us. Let us journey forward together, empowered by the knowledge that with God, all things are possible.

Heavenly First Love
By Ashley Thompson

A Living Relationship vs. Dead Religion:

> *"When I was a little baby you rocked me to sleep with the sweetest lullabies, when I was a girl you romanced me with toys and flowers, and when I became a teenager lost in emotions and hormones you were my truest friend…"*
> —Ashley Thompson, *Romantic Rendezvous for the Soul.*

I grew up in church, but I didn't know God for several years. My first memories of church were of an old brick building in Nassau, Bahamas. At the tender age of three, I spent long hours crawling by my mother's stocking-covered legs. I filled coloring pages along with my siblings; I was completely oblivious to anything that was said during the sermons I sat through. The AC would blast frigid air into the room, and I felt uncomfortably cold. These are my first memories of church. There was nothing of Jesus in my heart. I knew we prayed over meals as a family, but I didn't know the God we were praying to. To my infantile mind, He was as identifiable as another galaxy. Still, He saw me there in that church and He knew me. The same way He knows you.

> *Now this is eternal life: that they may know You, the only true [supreme and sovereign] God, and [in the same manner know] Jesus [as the] Christ whom You have sent.*
> —John 17:3 (AMP)

In the western world, I learned that the word "know" implies intellectual understanding. While this is true, it is not the complete picture. It is incalculably *valuable* to learn of Him through scripture and renew our minds according to scripture (see Romans 12:2). However, God doesn't just want to be loved with all our mind, but with all our *heart, strength* and *soul* too (see Mark 12:30). For years, "to know" simply meant head knowledge for me. In ignorance, I implemented my simplistic understanding of the word "know" to *all* references in the Bible. However, the word "know" in John 17:3 "suggests a very close intimacy, just as a husband and wife are intimate in marriage (Genesis 4:1). It implies experiential knowledge, not theoretical." I could only go so far in my relationship with God with the limited head knowledge I had as my compass. (For deeper understanding, read What the Bible says about Experiential Knowledge of God (bibletools.org)

> *"The church is preached as an army, a hospital, a factory, a convention center, a teaching seminar, an evangelistic outreach and a thousand other misconceptions. While the church may be involved in all these aspects, none of these tell us what the church really is. The church is not an army; it is a family. We are not here to attack the world with the power of God; we are here to win the world with the love of God. Jesus came to bring us into the family of God..."*
> —Dr. James Richards, My Church My Family

Almost two years later, my family moved to a beach town in California, and we began attending another church. I liked this church better. It had a liveliness that was contagious. The church was full of lovable people who quickly made the acquaintance of my parents. The icing on the cake was that we lived across the street from the head pastor.

He was a gardener from South Africa and had a vibrant yard and a generous smile. He and his wife opened their doors to my siblings and me. I can still see his wife's perfectly coiffed butterscotch blonde hair, snow white smile, and the sparkle in her eyes. We could knock on his door almost anytime and go jump on his children's trampoline in the backyard. He was my first mental image of a pastor. He once risked his life to help save our kitchen from burning down.

Sometime later, he confessed to the board about having an internal struggle with immorality. In his integrity, he resigned from the position as head pastor. I didn't understand his sudden absence as a little girl, and I missed him. This was the first negative memory I have relating to the church.

My family and I continued to attend that church as we waited for a new pastor. It was there, in that dear church, that I had my first memorable encounter with the Spirit of God.

> *Jesus said, "Let the children come to me. Don't stop them! For the Kingdom of Heaven belongs to those who are like these children." And he placed his hands on their heads and blessed them before he left.*
>
> —Matthew 19:15 (NLT)

Worship took on a new joy for me. I could never remember raising my hands to God in my mom's church, but I recalled many moments of raising my hands at this church. I began to sense the presence of God, although I didn't know it was His presence at the time. I sang to God with all the knowledge my pure heart knew about Him. I would talk to Jesus about things throughout the week. My mom tells me that she was "impressed" with my prayers as a little girl. I didn't know Jesus was listening intently and was watching over me.

> *Now Samuel did not yet know [or personally experience] the Lord, and the word of the Lord was not yet revealed [directly] to him.*
>
> —*1 Samuel 3:7 (AMP)*

One morning during church, the presence of God's Spirit rested upon me. It was like liquid love was clothing me more than the dress on my body. I had this incredible sense of wholeness and tranquility. Every fear I had as a little girl who was painfully shy and had a stutter, vanished. The hovering presence of the Holy Spirit followed me outside of church. I remember knowing that what I was feeling wasn't from me but was from someone else. I didn't understand who this someone else was, for while my church talked about Jesus and God, there was no mention, as far as I remember, about the Holy Spirit.

I didn't know that God's Spirit was the one who hovered over the waters at the beginning of creation before God spoke life into being (see Genesis 1:2). I had no concept that Jesus was the One who baptized with the Holy Spirit (see John 1:33). Jesus promised it would be better if He went away so the Holy Spirit could come (see John 16:7). The Holy Spirit gives power to every believer to bear witness of the resurrection of Christ (see Acts 4:31-33). He also unites us as the body of Christ (see Ephesians 4:3-4). I had no real perception of his *immense* preciousness, wonderfulness and worth.

> *"Holy Spirit is so vital that without him we could not be a Christian, we could not walk in our destiny, or have an intimate relationship with God (which is the ultimate goal, remember the first New Testament commandment) … He is the power it takes to have intimacy with Jesus..."*
>
> —Brenda Cobb Murphy, *How I Fell into the Spiritual Realm and Decided to Stay*

One morning, I fell asleep while on a long drive with my family. I woke up from my nap and saw that my older sister, Azania, was awake. I smiled at her, finding her incredibly dear. She smiled back at me. I still recall how the morning sun glowed through the car windows. The first thought I had was that I wished I had candy so I could give it to her. This thought was totally uncharacteristic of me. Like the average six-year-old, I was mostly self-centered. But when I looked upon my sister, I felt a strong sense of *selfless* love toward her. I wanted to see her happy. If I had candy, I would have joyfully given her all of it. I sensed this newfound, strong love for her wasn't from me. It came from the Holy Spirit who was upon me. I can't accurately describe the amazing level of peace I was feeling.

> "Men are reluctant to pass over from the notion of an abstract and negative deity to the living God...An "impersonal God" -well and good. A subjective God of beauty, truth and goodness, inside our own heads –better still. A formless life-force surging through us, a vast power which we can tap –best of all. But God Himself, alive, pulling at the other end of the cord, perhaps approaching at an infinite speed, the hunter, king, husband-that is quite another matter. There comes a moment when people who have been dabbling in religion ('man's search for God!') suddenly draw back. Supposing we really found Him? We never meant it to come to that! Worse still, supposing He had found us?
>
> —C.S Lewis, Miracles

Sadly, because I had never heard of the Holy Spirit, nor did I know how to look for the signs and fruit of His character, I began to question His company, although I knew He was *wholly good* and *better than I deserved*. I felt I was loved by this unknown presence and that He loved those around me with the purest love I'd ever felt. But I also didn't recognize myself entirely when He was with me. I was used to living with an undertow of fearful selfishness guiding my actions. I thought I would become too *different* if He were to stay.

The beautiful presence of the Holy Spirit stayed upon me like a warm, healing hug. In my ignorance, I said, "I don't know who you are. I'm asking you to go away." After that, I couldn't sense His presence. I immediately felt like I had lost something good, but I also returned to the normal state I was used to. I liken my experience to an avid gossiper who stops the sin of talebearing only to find quiet tranquility boring. Sin can be addicting. For that person who is used to gossiping, the blessing of sudden harmony might fit like wearing unfamiliar clothes.

I had found the sense of unconditional love through the Holy Spirit's presence upon me to be too celestial for me. This was tragic. When I think of all the hardships, I could have avoided had I never asked the Holy Spirit to leave (so I could be normal), I can't help but mourn. If only I had been taught the right knowledge of who the Holy Spirit was in church, I would have embraced Him wholeheartedly as a child. I have experienced the willful or blind rejection of the Holy Spirit in some churches. I have compassion on all Christians who don't know this beautiful Person. I once read a quote that said something like, "religion is all man has left when the Holy Spirit leaves the building." I believe the reason why we have so many denominations and doctrinal differences (which sometimes causes separation, discord and disunity in the Body of Christ) is because the Holy Spirit is not fully welcomed.

Thankfully, I would later discover that the Holy Spirit never truly went away, although I couldn't feel His presence. He stayed with me but mainly only as I would accept Him. He worked with my faith rather than violating my free will.

Dead Religion:

> *No one can know a person's thoughts except that person's own spirit, and no one can know God's thoughts except God's own Spirit. And we have received God's Spirit (not the world's spirit), so we can know the wonderful things God has freely given us.*
> *—1 Corinthians 2:11-13 (NLT)*

I continued to go to church, and I believe I had some love for God in my heart, but I didn't *know* Him. I couldn't truly know Him without the Holy Spirit. Going to church became a religious activity. Because of a lack of knowing God intimately, I did the best to live my life up to the Christian standards I knew were expected. Unfortunately, like any attempt to live a spiritual life in the flesh apart from God, I failed. No one around me in the church seemed to possess the vibrancy of having a living, passionate relationship with God either.

Once I became a teenager, insecurity began piling up in my soul like dirty laundry. Gradually, through the subliminal messages of society, I developed a low sense of self-worth. By this time, I had also gone through sexual molestation and years of teasing from peers. My father moved away to start a boating business in the Bahamas, and I hardly saw him over the next three years. My eldest sister, Ashanti, who had been like a second mother to me, moved away too. My family felt broken which made my inner world unstable.

The core group of my family moved to Florida to be closer to my dad. Despite my father's attempts to be present through his visits, his constant presence was *needed*. Having him with us sporadically wasn't sufficient. Our family suffered. I felt like a fish out of water in Florida, and I cried many times. My father's business began losing money and soon my family and I were within the poverty line. This created many problems.

Because I didn't know God, I didn't have a proper outlet for my pain, so I stuffed my emotions to hide my hurting heart. I didn't throw wild parties, enter sexual relationships, or try drugs. I vaguely discerned the unction of the Spirit of God talking me out of these things I would have otherwise probably succumbed to. He would influence me whenever I'd allow Him.

My coping mechanism of choice became *food*. At 15, I became obese. I dealt with stifling depression. I saw myself as ugly and unworthy to receive God's love. I was mostly a loner at school and to protect my hidden aches, I became verbally aggressive with those closest to me so they wouldn't discover my pain. Instead of revealing my deep wounds, I hid behind a wall of sarcasm. My meanness made me feel self-condemned. I *wanted* to be kinder to those I loved, but I allowed my inner hurts to harden me. However, God was faithful to pursue me in the gentle ways he knew best.

> "Therefore, look! I will now allure her. I will make her go out to the wilderness, and will speak to her heart."
> —Hosea 2:14 (ISV)

A Turning Point

> *I led them with cords of human kindness, with ties of love. To them I was like one who lifts a little child to the cheek...*
> —Hosea 11:4a (NIV)

The kindness of God began illuminating my night sky like glittering stars. My father walked away from his fishing business after facing a perilous tropical storm. He described hearing angels sing around him as his ship miraculously turned away from crashing into rocks. God told him He saved him to care for his family.

My father met us in Florida and together, we moved back to California. An invisible weight lifted off my shoulders. Our family seemed securer now. Ashanti came to live us again and she was full of zeal for God. She spoke about God like he was personally involved in her life. I was drawn to her like a moth to light.

She began gathering the family for devotionals. These meetings began to glue our family back together.

> "If a man has only correct doctrine to offer me, I am sure to slip out at the first intermission to seek the company of someone

> who has seen for himself how lovely is the face of Him who is the Rose of Sharon and the Lily of the Valley. Such a man can help me, no one else can."
>
> —A.W. Tozer

One morning I went into the garage, and I saw Ashanti was kneeling on the ground. She was bowing in prayer with only her phone as a light. The image of her having private time with God burned in my mind like sunlight to my eyes. Seeing her spend hidden time with Him inspired me tremendously. I remember her describing later how Jesus would rise early to fellowship with God in prayer (see Luke 6:12-13). One of the Song of Ascents lyrically cries out *"I long for the Lord more than sentries long for the dawn, yes, more than sentries long for the dawn" (Psalm 130:6a NLT)*

Months passed and although I had a desire to know God, I didn't enter a committed relationship with Him. I wasn't fully ready to give my life to Him like a bride vowed to give herself in marriage. I had been dating Jesus and enjoying his pursuit. I experienced pockets of his goodness and would taste samples of his kindness, but I never dedicated myself to him. As a result, I couldn't receive the blessings of covenant.

> "I want you to love me. I want you to trust me enough to let me love you, and I want you to stay here with me so we can build a life together. That's what I want."
>
> —Francine Rivers, Redeeming Love

At sixteen, I finally reached a point where I was willing to give my life *completely* to God. As I was listening to a sermon, I felt the tangible presence of the Holy Spirit again. I realized He was always there, but he had respected my request that He "go away." I surrendered my life at that moment, "I'm so sorry I've been ignoring you Jesus. Please forgive me for my sins. Come into my heart and be my *Lord* and *Savior*."

God opened my eyes spiritually, and I saw what looked like white, translucent rain falling through the ceiling. I experienced a cloud of peace in my heart. The greatest miracle of my life took place—I was born again (see 2 Corinthians 5:17). I also believe that the Holy Spirit filled me. He was no longer limited to following me on the outside; He now indwelt within me. Great transformation began taking place after that moment.

A Transforming Relationship

> "Christianity that isn't supernatural is superficial."
> —Unknown

> *"I promised you my love and entered the covenant of marriage with you. I, GOD, the Master, gave my word. You became mine. I gave you a good bath, washing off all that old blood, and anointed you with aromatic oils. I dressed you in a colorful gown and put leather sandals on your feet. I gave you linen blouses and a fashionable wardrobe of expensive clothing. I adorned you with jewelry: I placed bracelets on your wrists, fitted you out with a necklace, emerald rings, sapphire earrings, and a diamond tiara."*
> —Ezekiel 16:9-12 (MSG)

I began to sense the promptings of the Holy Spirit. I was guided to create a spiritual mind calendar where I put down purposefully things to do every day that would help me abide in Christ. Most of these things included prayer and Bible reading. I began by studying the fruit of the Holy Spirit in Galatians 5, and I limited my television watching. Please keep in mind, I felt led by the Holy Spirit to do these things. No one from the outside instructed me in this, so it wasn't "legalistic."

I prayed to Jesus to wake me up early to spend time with him before I did anything else. The very next morning, I woke up at 5 am, feeling an invisible hand on my arm. I even felt the fingers of this invisible hand. I opened my eyes and discerned the message of the Lord, "It's prayer and study time." For the next year, I would wake up almost every morning to be alone with Jesus. I read through the entire Bible.

The Holy Spirit led me through a process of sanctification. I began to sense what pleased God and what displeased him. I fully gave myself to Him, treasuring Him above all others.

As I dwelt in his presence, my heart began to heal. I was supernaturally delivered from a demon of anger that was sitting on the hurt in my soul. Now that the hurt was gone, the demon had left. I'm not sure if God kicked it out or if it left on its own. I literally felt an empty space in me where the anger usually was. I gave up my old life and accepted that I was a new creation in Christ. I no longer tended to give in to sinful anger. I began to overlook offenses and become a peacemaker. I no longer gave curt answers that cut my family. I now offered gentle words that turned away wrath (see Proverbs 15:1, NIV). The insecurities that once crippled much of my life began peeling away. As I received the love of God, I began to love myself and take care of my body. Within a year, I was at a balanced weight.

Not only did I love myself, but I *liked* myself. As a result, I gave that gracious love to others. My mind was slowly becoming a beautiful garden. I no longer had dark thoughts. Divinely inspired images began filling my mind, and I started having "visions" of the kingdom of heaven. I journaled some of these down in my book, *Visions of Celestial Love*.

> *"If you [really] love Me, you will keep and obey My commandments. And I will ask the Father, and He will give you another Helper (Comforter, Advocate, Intercessor—Counselor, Strengthener, Standby), to be with you forever— the Spirit of Truth, whom the world cannot receive [and take to its heart] because it does not see Him or know Him, but you know Him*

> *because He (the Holy Spirit) remains with you continually and will be in you.*
>
> —*John 14:15-16 (AMP)*

The Lord began stressing the importance of my obedience. The first relationship God repaired was with my father. God taught me that no matter how I didn't want to do what my father asked, I was commanded in the Bible to honor him. It was hard at first, but as I died to pride, I began walking in joyful obedience. My father and I developed a closer relationship. He began buying me presents at random and taking me on father-daughter dates. I went from a begrudgingly obedient child to a *willfully* obedient child. The Lord would inspire me to cook dinner for my family, clean the garage (although I hated doing so, especially since there were spiders), and *serve* them with my whole heart.

One night my eldest sister told me to not sleep on the couch. I liked sleeping on the couch because I could see the stars through the large windows. As I was drifting off to sleep on the couch again, the Lord reminded me of Ashanti's words. I frowned but spread a blanket on the floor and slept. In the morning Ashanti asked me why I was snoozing on the floor. I responded, "Because you told me not to sleep on the couch." She gave me a pleased smile and then said, "You can sleep on the couch (from now on)." God was showing me what it was like to grow in, "wisdom and in stature, and in favor with God and man" like Jesus who willingly *obeyed* his parents as a teenager (see Luke 2:51-52, NIV, emphasis added).

Miracles began happening in my life. I think it's important to note that I didn't chase miracles. I pursued knowing God. Miracles are a result of the presence of God. One morning after spending time with God, I proceeded to politely excuse myself. "Father, I'm hungry and I think I will watch TV." After making breakfast I tried to watch TV on two different televisions, and nothing was working. I checked the plugs and connections, and everything was set up right. There was no reason for the televisions to be showing static.

I went to the family computer and tried to watch shows on YouTube, but the internet wasn't "working." Then I got a small impression from the Holy Spirit to visit a ministry website by one of the ministers I enjoyed listening to. It worked immediately! It was like God was saying, "I'm enjoying your company. I want to spend more time with you."

One day, I was taking a shower and as it was ending, I realized I had left my drying towel on the sink counter which was past the commode. I didn't want to drip water on the floor, so I thought to lean on the towel railing and reach for my towel. I felt the Holy Spirit tell me, "Don't do that. The railing is unstable." I disregarded his impression, unsure if I had heard from Him and leaned on it anyway. It gave way and I began falling fast. I could have seriously gotten hurt, but I felt an invisible presence catch me and slowly lower my body down to the floor! I still don't know if it was an angel or the Lord who caught me. I recall thanking the Lord multiple times for keeping me safe.

One night I heard the voice of God. It was so clear, my ears picked it up, but his voice wasn't projecting from the outside. His voice came from *inside* my heart! He told me, "Ashley, your rabbit is going to get sick and die." For years I had prayed for the health of my family (spiritual, mental, emotional and physical). I would include prayers for my rabbit, Floppy's, health as well. I patted my chest where I heard his voice and stood frozen in wonder. I had never heard God so clearly! At this point in my walk, Christ was dwelling in my heart by faith (see Ephesians 3:17, AMP). The Holy Spirit had done a beautiful job of making my heart a nice home for Jesus. At that time, Floppy was showing no signs of illness, but I began spending more time with her as I believed Jesus had spoken to me. I took her to the park a lot; I videotaped her and gave her extra kisses.

Sometime later, she began to show symptoms of sickness. She stopped eating and would make small painful noises. We took her to the vet only to find out that cancer had spread throughout her body and there was nothing the vet could do. My mom decided it would be merciful for us to allow the vet to put her out of her misery. I was the last one to hold Floppy and I remember her licking me on my nose as I reluctantly gave her to one of the assistants. I cried loudly as I left the veterinarian. As dejected and sad as I felt, I realized Jesus had warned me ahead of time so I wouldn't be shocked by her passing. He also did this so I could spend more purposeful time with her and have cherished times together. He cared enough about me to warn me so I wouldn't be devastated.

Religious Professionalism verses Relationship

> *"The longer we walk with Jesus, the easier it is for us to fall for the trap of professionalism."*
>
> —Jessica Koulianos

From a pure heart, I began praying to God to serve his people in church because of my love for Him. I was already familiar with serving my family, but I wanted to extend this to God's people. I offered to help in the nursery. Before long, I was serving in many areas of ministry as I proved faithful in the little things. I began to offer help to others out of the kindness of my heart, and I was asked to become a youth leader. Eventually, I was asked to teach Sunday School, join the prayer team, help with seasonal church clean-up, teach on Wednesday family nights, and serve in various other areas. Soon I was at church up to six days a week. I had no real boundaries. Whenever someone asked me if I could do something, I would say "yes."

Years later, I began to lose my deep, personal connection with Jesus. Instead of being a *lover* who serves, I became a loving *servant*. I was still doing virtuous things, but that core connection that had been so sweet, tangible and beautiful began to wither. I became a professional Christian. The original joy, peace and sense of strong love I once had was slowly fading and, in its place, insecurity, bitterness and works of the flesh began sprouting up. I remember complaining with the other main volunteers in church. We had a saying: "20% of the people do 80% of the work." I allowed myself to be stretched beyond what was within my heart to give. I knew something was terribly wrong when I felt no joy during worship! I think it's important to note that the church loved me as they knew how. I made good friendships and precious memories.

> *"We are told not only to avoid those calling themselves brothers while they are still living in sin, but also to avoid those having 'a form of godliness but denying the power thereof' (2 Timothy. 3:5, KJV). We, like the disciples, are to avoid the leaven of the Pharisees. In 1 Corinthians 1:17, Paul warned that the wisdom of words makes the cross of Christ to be of no effect… There are those who believe in Jesus; they are saved and are on their way to heaven. They just do not believe God can do what the Bible says He can—in their lives."*
> —Dr. James B. Richards, Grace the Power to Change

Gradually, a religious spirit entered my life, and I allowed it to supersede the Holy Spirit's guidance for me. I became indoctrinated in religious teachings that sounded right. I was so naïve at this stage that I believed every word that was spoken over the pulpit to me from sincerely wrong Christians. Slowly, my fire for God cooled. My youth pastor at the time once told me that he was concerned that I could fall into the trap of being too *heavenly-minded*. He said something like, "You can become so heavenly minded that you're no earthly good." Comments like that helped to smother the flame of first love I once had for Jesus. I began to question if I was indeed *too* spiritual. I stopped sharing the miracle encounters I had with Jesus and the ways He would speak to me. If nobody around me was experiencing God like this, then I wondered if I was out of place. I began to very *gradually* conform to the image of saints around me instead of allowing the Holy Spirit to transform me into the image of Christ.

Eventually, the religious spirit who was with me began surreptitiously swaying me toward self-condemnation. I began to forget what it meant to be washed in the cleansing blood of Christ. Over the next three years, I traded faith-righteousness for works-based righteousness. I no longer came to God in confidence grounded on the finished work of Jesus. Instead, I was coming with the offering of my own good deeds which never allowed me real peace because I never knew if I had done enough to please God. Old sinful habits began rising, and I found myself making selfish decisions like I once did after telling the Holy Spirit to go away as a child. Every time I failed to live up to scriptural commands, I felt guilty. I would try to live godly in my flesh, apart from grace, and inevitably fall short. This would lead to feelings of shame and then I would try again. It was a vicious cycle. I lived with a sense of distance from my heavenly Father. The enemy began telling me that God had left me because I wasn't good enough.

> *"The moment I start trusting in my righteousness, according to Galatians 2:21, the grace of God is neutralized. It stops working, Christ stops being able to affect my life. I am limited to my own ability to live righteous, God's ability no longer has access to my heart. This does not mean I will immediately fall into sin. Rather, it means, I will conquer only the sins that I have the ability to conquer… it means that I will eventually grow weary from doing good deeds, and that I will become bitter when things don't work out as they should. (See Hebrews 12:15)."*
> —Dr. James B. Richards, Grace the Power to Change

I was being oppressed by a religious spirit and didn't even know it. I began seeing God as a rigid taskmaster instead of my merciful, loving Father who gave up His Son to save me. I cried endless tears during those horrible years. Eventually, I began to crave the spiritual presence of God. When I was born-again, I felt fulfilled spiritually, but now I felt starved.

I was *desperate* to know the love of God again. I felt inconsolable. I longed to be with the One I loved again. I didn't understand why He felt a thousand miles away. A few times I shared my grief with other Christians and the answers they gave lacked substance. Once my sister even told me that it was normal to not have a close relationship with God. Soon, I began to feel so gravely depleted that I started seeking spiritual experiences with God apart from scriptural integrity. I began thoughtlessly placing more importance on having a spiritual encounter "with God" that I unintentionally overlooked warnings in his Word. This is dangerous. I believe many young people are seeking a spiritual connection and when they come into dry, religious churches; they don't experience the kingdom of Heaven, so they go to the occult instead. The enemy is all too eager to give them a taste of the kingdom of darkness.

The Wiles of the Devil

> *These people are false apostles. They are deceitful workers who disguise themselves as apostles of Christ. But I am not surprised! Even Satan disguises himself as an angel of light. So it is no wonder that his servants also disguise themselves as servants of righteousness.*
> —2 Corinthians 11:13-15a (NLT)

Unfortunately, I soon became deceived by mysticism cloaked as Christianity. This began shortly after I befriended a professing Christian who had an inordinate amount of warfare in her life. I remember eating with her at a restaurant with a big Hindu idol in the garden. She did several things that I wasn't completely at ease with, but she had a supernatural ability that was "attractive." I began to suffer with strange pains and a few Christians began expressing their unease regarding my relationship with her. Eventually, I asked her for some space.

I found myself worse off than before. Not only did I suffer with condemnation and feeling distant from the Lord, but I now struggled with spiritual warfare. I picked up an occultic book that I thought was Christian (it was loaded with scripture) and began reading it. My mom visited me and once she discovered it, she promptly told me that it was demonic. I threw it away but unfortunately; I had *believed* its words. That night, I woke up feeling unclean spirits in my room. I felt them hold my hands and feet down so I couldn't move. I couldn't even scream. Then, I felt one of them dump a garbage can full of little demons in the pit of my stomach. It was like large bugs were crawling on the inside of me. The demons that were pinning me down left but the ones inside of me remained. I lived in *terror* after that. My church didn't believe that Christians could be demonized so I felt abandoned.

I became even more desperate to be "near" Jesus again. I heard of a missionary school that was a month long, and I believed they could help me. They proclaimed that they believed and walked in the authority of Jesus through the Holy Spirit. Unlike my church, they were not bashful about miracles. I thought I had finally found like-minded believers and with some strain, I made my way to the school. This school had a mixture of spirits. The occurrences that happened there were not all from the Holy Spirit. I can say this with confidence and forgiveness. I remember seeing a large, flying serpentine spirit enter my quarters and then enter my body through the center of my forehead, which I now understand has to do with the "third eye." It was colorful and had a white glow. I felt pain as it went into me, and I felt weak afterward, but I accepted this spirit instead of immediately rebuking it because I believed it was from God. By this time, I had listened to and read enough twisted doctrine that I was very open to deception.

> *My people are destroyed from lack of knowledge.*
> —*Hosea 4:6 (NIV)*

This incident came shortly after reading one of the books the missionary school recommended. I went through fire tunnels at this school where anyone who professed to be "Christian" could lay their hands on me and speak a "blessing." Many of the people around me who went through these tunnels ended up shaking on the floor and laughing wildly. I was told this was a manifestation of the Holy Spirit but later I learned it was mostly likely the manifestation of a kundalini demon.

> *For if someone comes and proclaims a Jesus other than the One we proclaimed, or if you receive a different spirit than the One you received, or a different gospel than the one you accepted, you put up with it way too easily.*
> —2 Corinthians 11:4 (BSB)

The leaders of this school came from churches all around the world. I believed the spirits influenced them as I believed the religious spirit I encountered in my home church. Both were spiritually deadening.

The Glorious Gospel (Almost too-good-to-be-true news)

> *One Sabbath day as Jesus was teaching in a synagogue, he saw a woman who had been crippled by an evil spirit. She had been bent double for eighteen years and was unable to stand up straight. When Jesus saw her, he called her over and said, "Dear woman, you are healed of your sickness!" Then he touched her, and instantly she could stand straight. How she praised God!*
> —Luke 10:10-13 (NLT)

Shortly after returning home, I went through the darkest season of my life. I thought I was going to Hell and that there was no hope for my life. By the mercy of God, I met a lady from Africa who had begun attending my home church. She told me that the Lord had instructed her to mentor me. She believed in deliverance and if it were not for her, and the few Christians in my church who knew the real power of the Holy Spirit, I probably wouldn't be alive or sane today. As I told her what was going on with me, she started to fight the unclean spirits the best way she knew how: through prayer and fasting. She met with me on a semi-weekly basis. While some of her methods were questionably religious, she cared for me deeply. I was instructed to fast many times by her and to pray for hours sometimes. I began seeing two Christian counselors who specialized in deliverance from Southern California. One of them was Dr. Charles H. Kraft, the author of *Deep Wounds Deep Healing*. He believes that deliverance often includes soul healing as well as casting out devils. I loved his gentle approach. I received much freedom through the two prayer counseling sessions I had with him.

That year, the Holy Spirit, whom I felt I had betrayed the most by unknowingly accepting false spirits, instructed me to rest in His love. A woman I had never met before told me, "The Holy Spirit says you are the apple of his eye, and He wants you to rest in his love." Jesus had also given me a vision earlier of this. I was sitting on my bed and suddenly I saw a little girl in the dark. She was young and weak. Her body and heart were bruised, and she was holding in her agony because she felt unsafe. Around her were these large, grotesque monsters. I knew she was me. She lifted her arms to fight even though she was no match for these monsters. When I looked at her, I knew she wouldn't last but a few seconds. One of the demons moved his foot toward her and suddenly a bolt of lightning struck the earth from heaven and landed in front of her. Jesus appeared in the light and with one swift motion, He scooped up the little girl in his arms and she weakly rested her head on His shoulder. He extended the other hand and fire started shooting from his palms at the monsters. Once the fire hit them, they vanished. He then took this hand and gently laid it upon her back. The fire started coursing through her body and soul, but it didn't burn (like the burning bush Moses saw). I realized that this fire represented His truth and that He was lovingly burning away the demonic and religious lies I had believed. He held me tenderly and walked with me. In the vision, I was so frail, I couldn't even hold on to Him. All I could do was rest in His strength. The concept of *rest* was incredibly hard for me because I was so indoctrinated by religion. I was trying to earn my deliverance and freedom through continual repentance and fasting. Mercy and grace were so foreign to me. I had incredible difficulty believing the simplicity of the Gospel again.

The Runaway Bride

In that day [the Lord will deliver Israel from her enemies and also from the rebel powers of evil and darkness] His sharp and unrelenting, great, and strong sword will visit and punish Leviathan the swiftly fleeing serpent, Leviathan the twisting and winding serpent; and He will slay the monster that is in the sea...

Wrath is not in Me. Would that the briers and thorns [the wicked internal foe] were lined up against Me in battle! I would stride in against them; I would burn them up together.

Or else [if all Israel would escape being burned up together there is but one alternative], let them take hold of My strength and make complete surrender to My protection, that they may make peace with Me! Yes, let them make peace with Me!

—Isaiah 27:1, 4-5 (AMPC)

Looking back, I realize the length of my bondage was in part due to the religious teachings I had picked up from sincerely wrong Christians. I was trying to fight off the demons with my flesh instead of allowing the Holy Spirit to do it, just like I had been trying to earn the miracles of God through good works instead of trusting in Jesus' *finished work* we receive from God by grace through faith. I had to put my trust in his grace and not in myself. Religion tends to make God's people self-conscious instead of Christ-conscious.

Resting almost felt like suicide because the battle was so strong that I felt like if I dropped my weapons, then the enemy would have me for lunch. I had to trust God to fight for me instead of doing what I was doing which was fighting for myself... and losing. The journey was tough, but I began to relax in the unconditional love of God for me through Jesus. I learned to focus my gaze on Jesus and not on the raging wind and waves. No matter what the enemy said, I had to believe that nothing could separate me from the love of

God which was *in* Christ Jesus (Romans 8:39). I went through mind games and frightening attacks by the enemy for months. Slowly I learned to not wage war after the flesh but in the Spirit (see 2 Corinthians 10:3-5). Once I allowed the Holy Spirit to get involved, the enemy had no chance.

When the religious spirit would come and accuse me and tell me I deserved go to Hell for what I had done, I had to raise my voice in faith and say, "I am the righteousness of God in Christ. I don't get what I deserve, I get what Jesus deserves. I am perfectly loved and redeemed." I realized I couldn't *accept* God's deliverance if I continued to believe the lies of religion that I had to *earn* it. It was hard for me not to focus on my own failings but instead, gaze at the cross of Christ and count myself as being *in Christ*.

The Holy Spirit continually reminded me that I was loved and forgiven. I began to discern the unction of the Holy Spriit again and as a result, I followed His instructions. My spirit man became strong in the Lord and in the power of His might. My soul was healing from the unconditional love of God and the ministry of the Holy Spirit. I began to feel like myself again.

One day as I was listening to Andrew Wommack preach on the finished work of Jesus, I began to shake. I was sitting on my bed when this happened. As I shook, my mouth would spontaneously open, and it was like I kept voicelessly coughing out things. I didn't see anything leaving me, but I knew I was being set free. This lasted for several minutes. Once it was done, I thanked Jesus for delivering me.

The next year of my life was like paradise on earth. I was twenty-three when I went to Charis Bible college. (It was started by Andrew Wommack). There, I met the man of my prayers, my husband. (He was my first boyfriend.) God gave me favor, and I ended up staying at a bed and breakfast lodge on thirty acers of forest land. It was beautiful and had a sunroof, jacuzzi, fireplace, and a chef. All my furnishings were provided for. I had ample time to study the Bible and care for my soul. My tuition was taken care of. God gave me the wedding dress of my dreams for *free*! I wrote my first self-published book, *Visions of Celestial Love*. I made priceless memories. I tell my husband to this day that those twelve months were like heaven on earth. I began to experience the power of the Gospel and have close intimacy with Jesus again.

I think it's a tragedy that many churches in the Western world ignore the need for deliverance and many of them struggle to believe that Jesus paid for physical healing. I believe many churchgoers suffer their whole lives with hangups, pains and torments because the church fails to preach and believe the whole gospel (we can consider ourselves dead to sin, alive to righteousness, born-again, new creations who are coheirs with Christ). Like the synagogue lady who was bound for 18 years by Satan even though she attended service, many believers are bound and sitting in church pews year after year. In fact, the leader of the synagogue was mad when He healed the woman who had been bound. Jesus didn't reply passively but called out the hypocrisy of the leaders and their lack of compassion (see Luke 13:15-16). I have a dear friend who is full of the Holy Spirit who has experienced religious persecution like this. He was the one God used to cast a religious devil from me. The gospel cannot be mixed with religion otherwise it becomes ineffectual.

The Beautiful Church

> *For husbands, this means love your wives, just as Christ loved the church. He gave up His life for her to make her holy and clean, washed by the cleansing of God's word. He did this to present her to himself as a glorious church without a spot or wrinkle or any other blemish. Instead, she will be holy and without fault.*
>
> *—Ephesians 5:25-27 (NLT)*

The church is the beautiful bride of Christ. The church is meant to be like salt and light. I truly love the church, and I'm so grateful for the way my home church first introduced me to Jesus. I cannot put a price tag on all the dear memories I have with other believers in church. The church is precious, vital, and heavenly. I pray that the purity of the gospel will sift out all leaven from the church. The church has a divine calling. She is meant to radiantly display the *love* of God, and she is to bear witness to the *resurrection* of Jesus Christ through the *power* of the Holy Spriit and the truth of scripture.

Overall, my view of the church has gradually become more mature and more based in scriptural soundness. The church is my family. The church is my first taste of heaven. The church is a part of my eternal spirit because the church is the Body of Christ. And we are all parts of Jesus. If one part of the body is broken off, the whole body is now crippled. If one part of the body is bruised, the whole body is damaged as a result.

You are infinitely loved by Jesus. You are His bride. He gave up His very life to have you. He allowed His blood to be spilled to cleanse you. He allowed His body to be broken beyond recognition to heal you. He conquered the power of sin in the flesh for *you*. He overcame the devil, the grave, and all diseases so you wouldn't have to fight that battle apart from him (because it's a losing battle without Him). He defeated the greatest enemies of your spirit, soul and body so you wouldn't have to! He calls his bride to abide in Him, because apart from Him we can do nothing (see John 15:5). What a wonderful Lord, Savior, Husband and Friend. I pray reading my testimony and this book will not be fruitless in your life. I pray Jesus will heal any pains you have suffered through your relationship with the church. I pray you will blossom where you are in your current church or be led by the wisdom of our heavenly Father to the "right church (without carrying offense from your past church)." Ultimately my prayer is that we, the church, will be one as Jesus is one with His father, for this is the very prayer of Jesus for us (see John 17:21-23).

"Your life will be totally transformed when you learn to have a healthy relationship with a church. You will find the peace, security, friendship and joy that can only come from meaningful, healthy relationships with your brothers and sisters in the family of God."
—Dr. James B Richards, *My Church My Family*

From the Parking Lot to the Pulpit

By Dr. Ebony Michelle Collins

(All scriptures were taken from the New International Version of the Bible)

The deafening sound of gravel crunching beneath my tires as I pulled up to the church matched the turmoil in my stomach. Each rotation of the wheels echoed the nervousness in my heart. Finding a parking space, I turned off the engine and sat there, gripping the steering wheel tightly. The familiar sanctuary of the church felt more like a battlefield with eyes, judgment, skepticism, and whispers weighing heavily on me. As a woman of God about to step into a space where my presence and voice were often unwelcome, the weight of centuries of tradition pressed down on me. The sun was shining brightly, casting long shadows across the church grounds, but the brightness outside contrasted sharply with the heavy atmosphere that awaited inside. Every step I took seemed to echo the doubts and reservations of those questioning my calling and place in the pulpit.

I took a deep breath, my hands trembling as I reached for the door handle. The cool air outside did little to calm my nerves. This church, once a place of solace and community, now seemed to loom over me with an oppressive silence. I steeled myself, reminding my spirit that my calling was greater than my fear. Every step towards the entrance felt heavy, each footfall echoing the battles fought by countless women before me who dared to challenge the status quo.

Inside, the murmurs of the congregation mingled with the faint sound of the organ playing softly in the background. Heads turned, eyes widened, and conversations hushed as I walked down the aisle. It was as if my mere presence disrupted the sanctity of their space. I could feel their gazes piercing through me, filled with a mix of curiosity, doubt, and even disdain. Yet, amidst the sea of unfamiliar faces, there were a few kind eyes silently offering their support and encouragement.

Taking my place at the podium, I felt the weight of the moment. This was not just about me; it was about every woman who had ever felt silenced, every person who had been told their voice didn't matter. My heart pounded as I opened my Bible, the pages worn and familiar and tabbed by my spiritual mother, offering a sense of comfort. I prayed silently for strength and wisdom, for the right heart posture to bridge the gap between tradition and the truth of God's inclusive love.

As I began to pray silently before I began my prayer to the congregation, my heart wavered, but I found steadiness in my faith. I prayed for hope, deliverance, and love of a God who sees beyond gender, who calls each of us by name to serve in our unique ways. I remembered stories from Scripture, highlighting the often-overlooked women who played pivotal roles in God's plan. The initial resistance was overwhelming but as I continued, I could feel walls beginning to crack and my mind began to be restored by GOD.

I believe the journey to acceptance and equality within the church is long and fraught with challenges. Deep-rooted traditions and beliefs resist change, but with every step forward, we pave the way for a more inclusive and loving community. The church should be a sanctuary for all, a place where every voice is heard and valued, where the image of God is seen in every person, regardless of gender.

For a moment, I feared that my words had fallen on deaf ears. Slowly, a single AMEN echoed through the room, followed by another and another, until the entire congregation bellowed HALLELUJAH! Tears welled up in my eyes as I realized that the seeds of change had been planted. The road ahead would not be easy, but this moment was a testament to the power of GOD.

As I stood before the congregation, I felt the unspoken tension. My journey from the parking lot to the pulpit was a spiritual and emotional battle against invisible barriers. Each step defied the obstacles placed before me and countless other women in ministry.

As I reflect on my life, memories of past struggles and triumphs flashed through my mind. The countless hours spent in prayer, the nights of wrestling with Scripture, and the moments of pure revelation and joy in the presence of God—all these experiences had led me to this point. Yet, the journey was far from over. I knew that standing before this congregation meant confronting not just personal fears but also societal prejudices and long-held misconceptions about women's roles in ministry.

When I entered the sanctuary, I was greeted by familiar faces, some smiling warmly, others looking on with a mix of curiosity and skepticism. The church, with its high ceilings and stained-glass windows felt both like a place of refuge and a battlefield. The pulpit, which had always been a symbol of authority and divine calling, now challenged me to prove that I was worthy of standing behind it.

The unspoken tension was palpable. It wasn't just about me; it was about every woman who had ever felt called to serve God in a capacity that tradition had not always endorsed. It was about breaking down the barriers that had kept so many talented and anointed women from fully exercising their gifts.

As I made my way to the front, I felt the support of those who believed in me and the resistance of those who did not. Both forces propelled me forward.

Taking my place at the podium for some announcements, I took a deep breath and looked out over the congregation. I could see the faces of young girls, eager and hopeful, looking up to me as a role model. I could also see the faces of older women, some of whom had faced similar battles in their own lives, offering silent encouragement. And then there were the men, some supportive, and others clearly uncomfortable with my presence in this leadership position.

In that moment, I realized that my journey was not just about me. It was about paving the way for future generations of women in ministry. It was about showing that God's call knows no gender and that the Holy Spirit empowers all who are willing to serve, regardless of societal expectations. My heart swelled with a mixture of fear and determination as I began to speak.

"My brothers and sisters in Christ," I began, my voice steady despite the butterflies in my stomach, "we are here today not just to hear words but to experience the living Word of God. We are here to break down the walls that divide us and embrace the fullness of the gifts God has bestowed upon His people."

As I spoke, I could feel the atmosphere in the room begin to shift. The tension was still there but mingled with a sense of anticipation and openness. I shared my journey, the challenges I had faced, and the unwavering faith that had brought me to this point. I spoke of the many women in the Bible who had answered God's call and how they had been used mightily for His purposes.

"God does not look at our outward appearance or our gender," I continued, "but at our hearts. He calls us to serve Him with all that we are and to use the gifts He has given us for His glory. Today, I stand here as a testament to His faithfulness and as a reminder that His call is for all of us."

By the time I finished, the tension had given way to a sense of unity and purpose. The congregation rose to their feet in applause, not just for me but for the message that we were all called to embrace. The journey from the parking lot to the pulpit had been difficult, but it was worth taking. For in that moment, I knew that the barriers were beginning to crumble, and a new path was being forged for all who would come after.

The challenges I faced were not unique. Many women endured similar struggles of dismissal, disrespect, and undervaluation. Despite these obstacles, the undeniable calling of God on our lives persevered.

From an early age, I felt a powerful sense of purpose, a divine mission placed upon me. Yet, as I navigated my journey, I found myself constantly battling against a society that seemed determined to undermine my potential. My experiences of dismissal were all too common among women. In professional settings, my ideas were often overlooked or attributed to male colleagues. The frustration of being spoken over or having my contributions minimized was a recurrent theme. Each dismissal was a stark reminder of the gender biases entrenched in our societal and professional structures.

Disrespect, too, was a familiar adversary. It came in many forms, from subtle condescension to overt hostility. I recall countless instances where my competence was questioned simply because of my gender. In meetings, my qualifications and expertise were frequently scrutinized in ways that my male counterparts never experienced. This disrespect extended beyond the workplace into personal interactions, where societal expectations often dictated that my value was tied to traditional roles and appearances rather than my abilities and achievements.

Undervaluation was perhaps the most insidious challenge. It manifested not only in the form of unequal pay and limited career opportunities but also in the pervasive attitudes that sought to diminish my worth. I was constantly reminded that my contributions, no matter how significant, were often seen as less valuable than those of men. This was evident in the lack of recognition and advancement opportunities afforded to women, which only reinforced the belief that we had to work twice as hard for half the reward.

Despite these pervasive challenges, the calling of God on my life remained a guiding force. My faith provided a source of strength and resilience, reminding me that my worth was not defined by societal standards but by divine purpose. It was this unwavering belief in God's plan that fueled my perseverance. Each setback became a steppingstone, each obstacle an opportunity to reaffirm my commitment to my calling.

I found solace and inspiration in the stories of other women who faced similar struggles and overcame them through faith and determination. These women, often unsung heroes, demonstrated that resilience and conviction could transcend societal barriers. Their journeys mirrored my own, providing a sense of solidarity and shared purpose. We were part of a larger narrative, one that stretched beyond individual experiences to encompass a collective struggle for recognition and equality.

In the face of dismissal, I learned to assert my voice with confidence and clarity. I sought out mentors and allies who valued my contributions and offered support and guidance. This network of support was instrumental in navigating the professional landscape, providing both practical advice and emotional encouragement. By surrounding myself with individuals who recognized my potential, I was able to counteract the negativity and build a foundation of self-assurance.

Confronting disrespect required a different approach. It meant standing firm in my convictions and refusing to be diminished by others' perceptions. I learned to address disrespect head-on, challenging prejudices and advocating for myself and other women. This often-involved difficult conversations and uncomfortable confrontations, but it was necessary to dismantle the ingrained biases that perpetuated disrespect. By consistently demonstrating my competence and integrity, I gradually earned the respect that had initially been withheld.

Undervaluation was perhaps the most challenging to overcome, as it was deeply rooted in systemic inequalities. However, I chose to focus on the intrinsic value of my ministry and the impact it had on others. I sought out opportunities to reach women, ensuring that I was hearing from God. Additionally, I became an advocate for equal opportunities and fair treatment for women and children, being an advocate by creating environments where women and children were valued and celebrated in Christ. During the early 2000s and earlier years, women in ministry faced significant tension. Despite societal strides in gender equality, the church remained a stronghold of traditionalism, sexism, and patriarchal structures. Women called to preach, teach, and lead encountered resistance that was deeply entrenched in historical and cultural norms. The pulpit, a place where God's word should flow freely, was often off-limits simply because of gender. This period marked a pivotal time of both challenge and change for women in ministry.

The resistance to women in ministry was multifaceted. Many denominations and congregations adhered to interpretations of scripture that emphasized male leadership, often citing passages such as 1 Timothy 2:12, which says, "I do not permit a woman to teach or to assume authority over a man; she must be quiet." These interpretations were used to justify excluding women from pastoral roles and other leadership positions within the church. This exclusion was a matter of policy and a reflection of deeply ingrained cultural and theological beliefs.

Women who felt called to ministry often faced a difficult path. They had to navigate a landscape where their calling was questioned, and their capabilities doubted. Many experienced a profound sense of isolation and frustration. Despite their clear gifts and dedication, they were often relegated to roles considered more appropriate for women, such as children's or women's ministries. While these roles are valuable, the restriction of women to certain types of ministries limited their ability to exercise their gifts and fulfill their calling fully.

The tension was not just external but also internal. Many women struggled with feelings of self-doubt and internalized the messages they received from their churches and communities. They wrestled with questions about their own worthiness and legitimacy as leaders. A lack of female role models in ministry compounded this internal conflict. Without visible examples of women leading from the pulpit, it was difficult for many to envision themselves in such roles.

However, the early 2000s and earlier also saw the beginning of significant shifts in attitudes towards women in ministry. The rise of feminist theology and the work of theologians who advocated for a more inclusive interpretation of scripture began to challenge the traditional views. These theologians argued that the restrictive interpretations of scripture did not reflect the broader biblical narrative, which includes numerous examples of women in leadership roles, such as Deborah, Esther, and Phoebe.

Churches and denominations began to re-examine their policies and practices. Some started to ordain women and appoint them to pastoral positions. This was often met with resistance and controversy, but it also opened the door for more women to pursue their callings. Seminaries and theological schools began to see an increase in female students, many of whom were determined to break through the barriers they faced.

The support for women in ministry also grew within the broader Christian community. Advocacy groups and networks were established to support and mentor women pursuing ministry. Conferences and workshops provided opportunities for women to connect, share their experiences, and receive encouragement. These networks played a crucial role in helping women to persevere in their callings and find avenues to use their gifts.

Despite the progress, the journey for women in ministry was far from over in the early 2000s. The tension between tradition and change continued to play out in many churches and denominations. Women still faced significant challenges, and the path to full acceptance and equality in ministry was often slow and arduous. Yet, the early 2000s marked a period of important breakthroughs and the beginning of a more inclusive approach to church leadership.

While traditional and patriarchal structures continued to pose significant barriers, the period also saw the emergence of new voices and movements advocating for gender equality in the church. The struggles and perseverance of women during this time laid the groundwork for future generations of female ministry leaders. As the church continues to evolve, the contributions of these pioneering women will remain a vital part of its history and ongoing transformation.

The struggles of dismissal, disrespect, and undervaluation are all too familiar to many women. Yet, through faith and God's will, we can overcome these obstacles and fulfill the divine calling on our lives. Our journeys are not solitary but interconnected, forming a tapestry of resilience and determination. By supporting one another and advocating for equality in churches, we can create a world where every woman's worth is recognized and supported in ministry.

Healing from internal wounds caused by years of marginalization and rejection was essential. Embracing my calling required immense courage and faith. The journey from the parking lot to the pulpit was about overcoming external barriers and healing internal wounds.

Marginalization and rejection can leave deep scars that influence how we see ourselves and the world around us. These internal wounds often lead to feelings of inadequacy, self-doubt, and fear. However, healing is possible through faith and trust in God's plan for our lives. Psalm 147:3 tells us, "He heals the brokenhearted and binds up their wounds." This assurance from Scripture reminds us that no wound is too deep for God to heal.

For years, I felt like an outsider, constantly struggling with feelings of rejection. These experiences made it difficult to believe in my worth and potential. However, God had a different plan. God was Healing My Focus in Life. He saw beyond my scars and knew the purpose He had for my life. Jeremiah 29:11 provides a powerful reminder of this truth: "For I know the plans I have for you," declares the Lord, "plans to prosper you and not to harm you, plans to give you hope and a future." Embracing this promise required immense courage and faith. It meant letting go of past hurts and trusting that God's plans were indeed for my good.

GOD HEALED MY FOCUS!

About Author Ebony Michelle Collins

Dr. Ebony Michelle Collins was born in Augusta, Georgia, the city renowned as the "Home of the Masters." As the only child for the first decade of her life, she eventually welcomed a younger sister, born ten years later. Dr. Ebony pursued her education with determination, earning a bachelor's degree in Sociology and a certification in Grant Proposal Writing. A devoted servant of Christ, Dr. Ebony Michelle has always been passionate about advocating for foster children and women. Her mission is to spread the "Good News" of Christ wherever she goes, touching lives globally.

In 2022, Dr. Ebony faced a sudden and profound challenge when her physical sight was altered. Rather than succumbing to adversity, she redirected her focus and energy toward becoming a powerful voice for abandoned children and their needs. This life-changing experience deepened her empathy and compassion, driving her commitment to ensure that foster children and women receive the support and advocacy they deserve. As a passionate advocate for children in foster care, Dr. Ebony is dedicated to fighting child hunger within the system and helping women find their purpose in life. Her unwavering spirit and determination to stand in the gap for those in need have made her a respected figure in the community.

After becoming a foster parent, Dr. Ebony quickly gained recognition for her innovative and effective approach to supporting children in foster care, particularly those with disabilities. Serving as a liaison between the state and families, she has been instrumental in bridging gaps and fostering positive outcomes. Her dedication to her mission led her to pursue a certification in Christian Counseling, and she was honored with an Honorary Doctorate in Christian Humane Letters from her beloved seminary.

In 2023, Dr. Ebony Michelle was awarded the prestigious Joseph R. Biden Jr. Presidential Lifetime Achievement Award, recognizing her lifelong commitment to service. Throughout her journey, Dr. Ebony Michelle has been involved in numerous initiatives aimed at improving the lives of foster children. She has opened her home to sibling groups, created growth opportunities for children in foster care, and provided a haven for those with learning challenges. Her compassion for the well-being of foster children and women is the driving force behind her advocacy, as she works directly with foster agencies to help children overcome trauma and transition to better lives. Dr. Ebony Michelle Collins is walking in her purpose, with a lifetime of dedication to the community ahead of her. Guided by her faith, she allows God to heal her focus and continue her mission of compassion and advocacy.

Burnt Alive

By Leah Clement

(All scriptures were taken from the New International Version of the Bible)

The identity of the bride is generally considered within Christian theism to be the church or the body of Christ with Jesus as the bridegroom as the head. Paul in the book of Ephesians 5:22-33 compares the union of husband and wife to that of Christ and the church. It is a favorite ecclesiastical analogy.

As a bridegroom would love his bride, Christ demonstrated the ultimate level of love by death in the most dishonorable manner according to the will of God as stated in John 3:16, "For God so loved the world that he gave his one and only Son, that whoever believes in him shall not perish but have eternal life." In the same way as the husband and the wife become one flesh, so every fabric of our being must be enveloped in Christ so that we can become one with Him.

As we traverse in the rhythmic pulsations of time, our mortal life becomes inevitably subjected to challenges; nevertheless, we have confidence in the advocacy of the Father to give us the potential to overcome. Just as the bride makes herself ready for her husband, so we must also live in a place of sacrificial readiness in accordance with Rev 19:7, "Let us rejoice and be glad and give him glory! For the wedding of the Lamb has come, and his bride has made herself ready."

I am in a place now with a resident peace in my heart where this individual bride can begin to disseminate the entirety of a most devastating ordeal that resulted in immediate ex-communication. This was my house of fellowship which defined my entire world at the time, an organization that now boasts of a monthly membership of approximately 8.8 million active members.

It is my quest to inform others who have experienced a moral and ethical failure with the leadership of the church that regardless of the nature of the trauma they have encountered, which might be very painful and difficult to overcome, they can learn how to move forward with their life and the things of God.

The church is imperfect and flawed but may be in a perfect place in God and that may qualify them to assist us in overcoming church hurt.

I have learned to not let my hurt define my relationship with Christ. I have chosen and learned the importance of forgiveness, even when deeply hurt or in pain, which is the first step to healing. True forgiveness has helped me to release and remove all anger and bitterness from my heart that has been an impediment in my upward mobility.

The benefits of releasing trauma and pain caused by the church through the act of forgiveness are many, which includes greater emotional well-being, stronger relationships and a deeper sense of grace and mercy which overweighs trauma.

Religious organizations are hardly devoid of its share of shenanigans and idiosyncrasies amid the pursuit of the mark of the higher calling in Christ. Their actions, in many instances, resemble that of the Babylonian culture. The heart of man continues to be inundated with unspeakable wickedness and his imagination of his thoughts continues to be evil. So, it was in the days of the early church and so shall it be in the days of the coming of the son of man. (Genesis 8:21-22).

The spirit of some leaders in offices of these organizations would rise up against members of their flock in dealing with issues and they would, at times, act by virtue of their own justifiable decisions by their egoistic disposition commensurate with the regulations of their organization to engender "correction" rather than by any kind of scriptural validation to bring chiropractic adjustment to the lives of the individuals. Cronyism often fuels their "righteous indignation" that takes precedence over impartiality and that would unobjectionably be deleterious to an individual emotionally, spiritually and mentally and it brings the integrity of the leadership and the organization by extension into question.

This behavior is an indictment of the very function of divine order according to the scripture and can pierce and penetrate like arrows into the substructure of a person's consciousness and spirit. If their house is not built upon an uncompromisable internal foundation, a visceral hatred for the church can develop and subsequent repatriation to the alma mater of world-conscious dispositions. The leaders would be held accountable for standing in the way of the "transgressor."

My mother fully embraced the ideology and philosophy of the organization and that became the template from which she built her life and nurtured her kids. Because of her indefatigable conviction, at a tender age, I was indoctrinated into this controlled religion and cult-like community which turned out to be a deceptive pseudo-religion with spurious unscriptural teachings and did more damage to my psyche than truly nurtured and equipped. We were more than just church denizens but heavily involved in the activities of the organization. I existed in a state of hyper-vigilance, idolizing the elders of the church as if they were superior to me. Dreadful fear and idolatry of them had camouflaged itself as reverence and respect, but their dominance was manipulative and cruel which led to stress and dis-ease in my tripartite constitution which manifested itself as unresolved trauma up to adulthood.

My mother was well-liked and favored by the members of the church. The commendation she received from the members was a report card for our strict and well-mannered disposition at all times which was alluded to our initial acculturation and religious indoctrination as a characteristic function of the Law matriarch. At the age of eleven, I felt that I was erudite enough and vehemently debated the bible with my elders and juniors with insatiable passion.

For reasons that I learned and understood later on in my life, my parents separated, and I no longer had the safety and luxury afforded by a conjugal family unit. The circumcision of the family unit created an internal, as well as a socio-economic migration. I went from a place of abundance to a place of lack, and from having an abundance of food to depending on hand-outs to survive. My dad was an international offshore chef, the sole breadwinner, and my mortal pillar. His precipitous departure left a dangerous void within my soul.

After several years of separation from my father, my mother started another relationship -- this time with someone totally oppositional in disposition, mannerism and respect to my dad. A devout "born again" alcoholic with an erratic behavior *with and without* being inebriated was a novel experience that I did not handle very well. I was traumatized to the point of relatively being an introvert, and my mother seemed to be incognizant of the effect her companion's behavior had on my mental and emotional well-being but was rather engrossed in the limerence of her present heartthrob. Her concern was filling the void of my dad at all costs, and her new partner took precedence over the future welfare of my sister and me. These two metamorphic events signaled a new era in my existence.

Eventually, at age sixteen, I reluctantly sought refuge elsewhere to preserve my sanity and to accommodate the internal shift that was in transition. I had to prematurely bring closure to an era of having emotional and financial support and cognitive dissonance was not discounted for its traumatizing effects.

This unique and unexpected scenario bulldozed the door to my vulnerability which, on many occasions, could have had me killed.

I was now on my own and more exposed to a world that is unwittingly ferocious with no kind of preparation. I entered the world of work and that afforded me some sort of independence but deep inside, I was not looking for an intimate relationship but a genuine friendship of a male figure in the quest to supplant the care and attention that I was accustomed to by my father.

My physical attractiveness and pleasant disposition attracted many but seldom equated to the turmoil that was assassinating every fiber of my being on a quotidian basis. Seeking companionship when vulnerable is a recipe for disaster.

My first relationship experience at fourteen was with a member of the organization. We grew a special kind of bond I had never experienced before which made me feel supported, cared for, and understood. His presence in my life was constant until he found someone of his age to fulfill his sexual desires and darker pathologies, and he eventually got married to her. Although wounded, I understood his position and kept to myself, but it was a formidable task because his place of abode was proximal to mine. After a considerable hiatus, he began making his presence known in my life. His marriage was not working so I thought there was hope for me. We eventually became intimately involved but the guilt of adultery was like a thorn in his side. This incident was the catalyst for a series of misfortunes with men that followed.

Between the ages of seventeen and eighteen, I was violently sexually assaulted on a few occasions -- at one time by the son of a prominent proprietor.

None of these instances resulted from promiscuity. For someone who has had bad experiences with men from the beginning, the concept of lesbianism has never and will never take root in my consciousness but for years, I held a heavy prejudiced disposition.

The sum total of the short dark period of my life took a toll on me. I could no longer bear it and requested a meeting with an elder of the organization to make things right with God and start anew.

The council assembly was entirely male, with six members present, and they insisted on hearing every sordid detail of my encounter during the four-hour session. I experienced a water baptism at an early age, but this was a second baptism, not of the Holy Spirit and a holy fire but one of raging fire and brimstone. And if this wasn't enough, I was even crucified by the devastating actions of another elder whom I had loved and respected when he found out that I was statutorily raped. I was so horrified by his cruel behavior towards me that I could feel the arrows piercing into my head and heart. The ordeal experienced by the eldership of this religious organization was beyond devastating and so humiliating that it resembled a Nazi interrogation during the reign of Adolf Hitler that I read about a few years prior. I understand that whom God loves, He chastens and rebukes in love by those in authority; however, there was no display of love or forgiveness as immediate ex-communication, even with a letter of appeal, supplanted proper council for healing and restoration. Love seemed to have been metered out to a selected few.

It was way past the sunset hour when the meeting ended. Voracious, disappointed, and disillusioned, I was left to stand at the side of the lonely and dimly lit road opposite the organization's edifice to wait for public transportation to make my way home, fifteen minutes before the midnight hour. The meeting took a heavy toll on me which ushered me into another dimension, that on leaving the premises, I immediately crossed the streets without looking for oncoming vehicles and almost got run over by a speeding vehicle. I wistfully gazed as members hurriedly exited the building in their various modes of transport passing me by like I never existed without one single common courtesy to offer me a lift. I felt like a useless piece of filthy, old, and worn-out rag that nobody needed. I believed I had committed the most heinous and unpardonable crime in the universe. I felt as though the earth opened and swallowed my house as my haven, healing, refuge and fellowship in the only sanctuary I knew as long as I had cognitive ability was violently removed from my life in the blink of an eye. The hope which once anchored my faith evanescence like a breeze on the ponderosa.

Fortunately, God is not like man, and He cannot act outside the jurisdiction of His Word. Man, by virtue of his finite mentality and religion by extension, always seeks to define us based on the conviction of their five senses, whereas God always looks at the heart.

When leaders hurt their flock, it can aggressively modify the landscape of their spirituality and engender internal confusion and an impenetrable spiritual disposition to the Word of God again. It is a dangerous time for us but an opportune time for the enemy to utilize our minds as battlefields to justify the concept of persevering by way of Satanic systems that we once fellowshipped with. But God's grace is sufficient for us and in our weakness, He is strong.

Amidst the pain and devastation, some of the organization's principles were deeply ingrained in my mind. Although these principles became my survival mechanism, keeping me going for so long, they acted as a barrier, preventing me from being open to the true word of God that could bring change and restoration.

The unforgiveness I carried for years was a heavy burden that crushed my neck and a megalith in the pathway of my progress. It was a bitter pill to swallow.

Traumatic experiences of the past had taken a toll on my physiology and my ongoing battle with a host of diseases that I battled daily. I found myself nestled on a hospital bed having a near-death experience. My only visitor was my cousin who prayed with me and led me to Christ. This time, not from a ritualistic standpoint, but a true encounter with the *parakletos* (the Holy Spirit). I have read it on many occasions but for the first time in my life, I understood the meaning of a "peace that surpasses all understanding."

This was the beginning of my journey of forgiveness. An unprecedented peace and the feeling of a load lifting off my shoulder was an unfamiliar experience that would be etched in my memory forever. I left the hospital with a new sense of journey and freedom, for "if the son sets you free, you will be free indeed" (John 8:36). I cannot say that immediate, consistent prayer and counseling were initially instrumental in my healing and deliverance because, at the time, I was not subjected to such rationalizations. Conversely, over time, a level of healing took place within my soul. It was not until I began to fellowship at a full gospel gathering the unadulterated Word of God which is quick and powerful and sharper than a two-edged sword began to dismantle structures of the past pseudo-doctrinal belief systems in my mind; then healing truly commenced. Additionally, the expertise of world-renowned life coaches was sourced, and they were instrumental in making an indentation in my healing pilgrimage.

I am still in the process of healing and deliverance, but I have come a mighty long way.

Although life presents itself with many challenges that may seem insurmountable, my mantra remains, "with God all things are possible." (Matt 19:26.)

It follows, therefore, that we cannot allow ourselves to live in defeat or to be defined by our circumstances or the limitations of our finite mind. Instead, we should always internalize the fact that Jesus did a finished work, and we should walk in the principle of the finished work.

About Author Leah Clement

Born in Trinidad, Leah Clement's journey from a small island to global influence has been nothing short of extraordinary. Known to the world as "the impossible, fearless resilience Queen," Leah's indomitable spirit and unyielding faith have left an indelible mark on the lives of millions. Leah's unique approach to life, driven by her belief that "all things are possible with God," has often led others to label her as unconventional, crazy, or impossible. Yet, it is this very conviction—her immutable belief in the power of the Holy Trinity—that has fueled her remarkable success.

Leah's pursuit of excellence led her to become a certified international public and motivational speaker, trained by the legendary Dr. Les Brown and coached by Jon Talarico, the world's #1 success coach on connecting your mind, message, and million-dollar network. She is also a published international best-selling author, with her book *Mind Wellness Champions* available on Amazon.

As a champion of mind wellness and mental health, Leah has been featured on numerous global podcasts and was the keynote speaker on the *Rise to Greater Heights Network,* where she discussed cultivating a mindset for success, particularly concerning youth mental health. In addition to her speaking and coaching career, Leah is a legal executive with a distinguished background in law, having earned her education from the University of London and the Institute of Legal Executives (ILEX) with merits and distinction. She has served with distinction at some of Trinidad's most reputable law firms.

Leah is also an accomplished poet and the Founder/CEO of Red-Carpet Foundation, a non-profit organization dedicated to empowering others and instigating paradigm shifts through the collaborative efforts of a professional collective. She holds various leadership roles, including President of the Parent Support Group at her children's elementary school and Advisor and Host of various communities and groups. Leah's achievements have been recognized globally, with features in the 2022 Hoinser Queen's Magazine and Hoinser book, highlighting her as one of the 100 most influential and inspiring women worldwide. She continues her theological studies at Zion Christian Mission Center (ZCMC), where she has been enrolled since 2023.

Leah Clement is a beacon of resilience, fearlessness, and unrelenting faith. Her legacy of leadership, faith, and impactful storytelling is poised to inspire generations to come, through books, podcasts, publications, documentaries, and any other medium God chooses.

All Eyes Are On Us
By Lillie B. Randle

"Is that the van?" I asked my boys several times. I heard multiple horns along with the crunching of snow from nearby vehicles as they slowed down for the traffic light which was close to the corner of my residence. My anxiety gripped me tightly at this time. It led to me hollering from my bathroom while putting the finishing touches on my red and purple lipstick with a hint of brown and some light pinkish blush.

While rushing down the stairs while grasping the wooden rail carefully so as not to fall, I rambled off a series of instructions: "Get your coats on, turn these lights and television off, now! Mike, go upstairs and check the lights. Drew, go to the kitchen and dining room! Jordan and Joshua, let momma help y...." Beeeep, Beeeep! The horn blared in the distance, and I found myself running to the door in my red, suede furry-heeled boots, pushing children out the door, as a gust of zero-degree wind (like the days of Pentecost) almost floored me. I began prompting them to get to the gate with their assigned bags. Meanwhile, I am at the door locking up like Fort Knox.

The van showed up but wasn't close to the curb like usual. Giving the driver the benefit of the doubt, I thought he must be putting the step down.

Turning and almost falling downstairs, I saw the green church van, with its gold letters, as it flowed up the street with traffic. I did not have to ask my boys why they didn't get in.

"Mommy, are we going to church?" my youngest son demanded of me. Considering this had happened several times prior to this one, I held back the waterfall that was begging to come forth. I gave a loving smile and nodded yes, not knowing how determined the adversary was who was fighting against me using spiritual warfare. After gasping slightly, I cleared my throat and said, "We're going to go across the street and wait there."

Jordan replied, "But, isn't it cold?"

"It'll only be a few minutes; the driver had to go get another family first, is all." (This was my feeble attempt to convince my children and myself that this was indeed the case.)

I motioned to them, "Come on, now while there's no traffic."

We quickly and carefully crossed the street. I was standing in 18° weather, doing my best to not shiver, so my boys wouldn't realize just how cold it really was. Within a few minutes, I shared with excitement the van was coming. The boys and I began to wave, as it was an SOS to get the assistance we desired. We just wanted to go to church and worship. Our neighbor from across the street came out and asked if we were okay. I just simply nodded. By then, our church van was back at the traffic light. We were all smiles and started towards the curb to get on the van. The van beeped the horn. I waved for him to stop so we could get on.

Literally, I had to pull us all back so we didn't get hit. I thought the driver was going to stop because we had eye-to-eye contact. Even my children saw it. This hurt more than it usually did. On top of this, my neighbor was a witness.

He asked me, "So hey church lady, what did you do where your church don't want to pick you and your babies up no more? Must 'a been pretty bad."

I was extremely angry, disgusted, and completely embarrassed for myself and my children. I wanted to scream at and cuss this neighbor out, but I recalled how he brought my youngest, my escape artist, back in one-night last summer from the middle of the road around 11 pm.

Politely as I could, I timidly replied," No, sir, we did nothing! Have a blessed day!"

I waved and ushered my boys back across the street while answering even their probing questions. They wanted answers, also. I gently restated, "Babies, we did absolutely nothing wrong, and I don't understand why this happened. I guess we may have been a little too close to the road; that may have been my fault. I humbly apologize. Momma is deeply sorry."

I did what I thought was best. I took the blame so they wouldn't feel angry towards the church or the van driver. I even told them he may have had a bad day, and we were simply forgotten as we re-entered 377 Genesee Street. The warmth of our apartment greeted us kindly and tenderly. I told the boys to change from their church clothes.

Even though I wanted to, I wasn't ready to face the people at church. The anger seemed to permeate my very existence during that moment. I knew the van driver from when we were teenagers. We somewhat dated, and he was the Pastor's son. Just thinking about some of the things we did in and outside of the church makes me cringe. I had risked losing my soul because I allowed him to do unholy stuff to my fifteen-year-old body. I had needed to be known as the Pastor's son's girlfriend. His parents allowed us to talk on the phone because I was always respectful of them. We completed a few undisclosed sinful acts in the house of God. (Thank God, we never were completely intimate.)

Why was this man, who was supposed to be happily married and with his own family, was so nasty and coldhearted towards me and mine? I knew his wife and I were getting close and very friendly, but dang! I never told her about the past -- the shameful and misguided past of a teenager who severely lacked self-esteem with depression.

I wasn't quite sure what to do in this case. Who was I supposed to share this with? I just wanted my children to be raised up in the church where I started to trust God and made up my mind to stop sinning. I was going to live for Christ no matter what. Apparently, Lucifer had a different plan. He began to use the transportation department of that church, and we begin to miss Sunday after Sunday, then Wednesdays and Fridays, also. I wasn't making much money at that point in our life. Therefore, it was extremely difficult to get there. This disaster went on for a long while, well over a year.

No one inquired where we were and why we weren't coming as much or even how we got there when we did show ourselves. It always seemed like they were surprised to see us and yet happy we didn't fall off the planet, somehow.

The incident described above was one of several that took place for almost 2 years. We became lost in the shuffle of our church's everyday life. There were a couple of times my ex-Pastor, may God rest his soul, got involved and there was correction each time. So, during the almost two years of misery, we only got picked up successfully about 25% of the time when the driver was different, new, or the Pastor made them. The man, the Pastor's only child, whom I was most familiar with, was over the Transportation Department.

My children came downstairs, and I went upstairs to change out of my clothes and adjust my mood. I was upstairs for an hour. Yes, it took that long for me to get myself together. As I undressed, tears fell and anger came out. I repented and prayed and read Psalm 23. It seemed to help me as much as I allowed. I then came downstairs and fed my family a light dinner. Soon, I began to read to the boys Genesis chapter one for like the 30th time out loud.

I was sure the children were going to request a different scripture. I think they were just happy we were together and toasty. I taught them what I could from what I recalled from when I was a little girl. I prayed a lot at this stage of this trial.

After a little while of not attending church, I thought my children were missing their friends from church. I called the church, instead of the transportation number, and the Pastor answered. I clearly never expected that.

He inquired, "Daughter, where have you been? How are those boys? Are you okay?"

I didn't want anyone to get into trouble because I began to believe that maybe it was my fault. I had these children, and it was my responsibility to raise them. I could have been asking too much of the church. I wasn't sure what to say to my former Pastor. I somewhat felt like the church was against me and maybe he knew more than I thought.

A bit overwhelmed, I managed to reply nervously, "We…at home. They are fine. We are okay as we can be." Strangely, it didn't seem good enough. Pastor asked me when we were coming back. My reply was in reference to the line not working properly for transportation because I had been calling and no one came.

Well let's just say that for almost three months, unless we were sick and I actually didn't call, we got picked up.

Then slowly over about 4 months, it started again. The excuses were: We always came out late; we weren't ready when they got there. So, I soon started getting us ready two days ahead of time and prepped Mike to watch the door. This did not work for the most part because no matter what, we ended up at home 75% of the time and eventually 100% of the time.

I would sometimes have a few extra dollars and would get a cab or grab the bus. Well, when I did this, there was this rule: the way you come is the way you leave. I would even explain that I used my last to get here. I was told, "I guess you should have thought about that before you came!"

After such cruel and mean behavior, I felt like I was alone with my children, and we were being judged harshly because of my history of backsliding in and out of the church. I did not protest this treatment with other church members as I felt no one would sympathize with me. I was sure in the end, they would probably have made us feel worse. So, I just kept it all in. I kept praying. I started asking my parents and other members to get us. I would do my best to get to the door early or at least out the door on time. I didn't know we would be wearing people's patience out that I thought cared about us, at least that's how it felt. They all, at one point in time, would ask why we didn't utilize the transportation. I would give my explanation, and they suggested I try again. Once again, I am calling and calling, even in front of witnesses. Sometimes, as I noted, they came, but most times, they did not even come down our street. When it was nice out, we would be outside for an hour and nothing. Crying deeply within, I finally concluded that this was no longer our church home.

I don't remember the exact date it was, just that it was a Sunday morning. I got up around 6 am. I made breakfast. I saved up enough for a roundtrip cab ride to church. I was going to go to the church one last time with my children to see if my thoughts about this church were accurate. *Did they truly hate us? Were they being tricked by Satan?*

It had been almost 6 months since we had left without as much of a sneeze or boo! My children were telling me about how they did not want to go because of getting bullied before. This response totally caught me off guard. I asked them why they didn't say anything about it. The collective response was that I was already going through enough between their father and the church; they chose not to bother me. Now, I knew my adversary must really hate us.

Upon hearing this from my children, my heart broke. Finally, after I hugged my boys, we went upstairs and got ready for one final attempt to salvage our almost dead church relationship. I refused to give up without a fight.

Once we were all ready, I called the cab. We waited outside in the chilly autumn air. There were smells of dried maple leaves floating by in the crisp wind with the last of the monarch butterflies fluttering near the last of the red roses clasping to their lives, irony at its best. I gently smiled as the burnt-out tires of the cab pulled up. We trickled in and I clung deeply to the last of my faith. I thanked the driver for picking us up. He smiled via the rearview mirror. My boys couldn't quite settle down as we arrived 15 minutes later into the driveway over the crackle and pop of the stones and rubble under the weight of the cab as it screeched to a stop on the tar pavement near the front door of the church.

I gave the cabbie $15 and rushed my children from the vehicle. The driver moved quietly, yet quickly out of sight.

It was time to face the Eyes of Judgement. I moved slightly from the driveway towards the front doors. I prayed a quick prayer, gripped my Bible and looked up, "Lord help us!" We ventured into the house of prayer. We stood for a moment in the lower vestibule where there were a few families who recognized us. I stood as tall as 5' 4" could and braced for the impact because 'All Eyes Were On Us'. I let my boys go downstairs with specific instructions to say nothing to the mean people, other than *God is watching and ask my mommy, please*. I did this with a nod. They understood the assignment!

A beautiful sister approached me with multiple questions. I simply explained, "God will be the ultimate judge today and my vindicator. Now let me get to Christian Education." Upstairs, I went to the sanctuary. Everyone just stared after that. My boys and I had a mid-morning snack during the break. My children shared with me how their Christian Education went, as they wanted to know if they had to come back with worry in their eyes. This was the first time in a long time that we enjoyed morning worship, however, the people did not change. We weren't going to take it. We said our goodbyes and left, hopefully never to return, even as visitors. My children were between the ages of 3 and 9. It hurt us deeply to leave. For about two and a half years, we weren't connected to any church at all. I tried hard to keep up with leading them righteously, but I started to do my own thing. I would pray with my children and teach them scriptures here and there. Soon, I began to get lost in myself reverting to prayer every now and then. I was in a total backslidden condition.

God began to pull on my heartstrings to come back to him. I was in a relationship of sorts. My children were experiencing stressful times while I was living my choice. One day, I got involved with an old pastoral friend. We began to go back to church *somewhat*. I let go of a lot of people, places, and things. God asked me to help someone and then that pastoral friend excommunicated us both because of the individual God wanted me to help. I was like…what? She said the young person had evil intentions and was holding me back. I left them alone for a while. (Later down the road, we became friends again.)

One day, this individual and I went to pray by the river, May 26, 2012. We enjoyed the joy of the Lord and His grace and tender mercies. I decided it was time to go because it was my son's 12th birthday. We got on the bus. We were discussing where we were going to get off and at first, I agreed to the first stop, but I got an unction to get off at the stop around the corner.

Unknown to us, God had my current beloved Pastor waiting for us. The beautiful Pastor of my current church home, Purpose Driven Ministries, was outside and ministering to a young lady. We were walking past, and I heard something familiar-- *prayer* and the Word of God being shared with someone on the street. I had not heard this in an extremely long time. I knew it was God. So, we felt compelled to stop and the presence of the Lord was in the midst.

I have matured in God's word by fasting, praying and studying the Word of God. God has reassured me that he has my oldest, and I am grateful for it. I can only pray that you come to know this for yourself: Hold fast to God and never let go because He has never let go of you. He loves you the most and that is a fact.

About Author Lillie B. Randle

Lillie Randle is a Kingdom-preneur, devoted mother of four, a loving aunt, cousin, sister, and a proud grandmother (affectionately called Yaiya & Yaiga) to nearly a dozen grandchildren—two of whom are yet to be born. Her unwavering commitment to her family has always been her driving force, often working multiple jobs to provide for her loved ones.

Through the grace of Almighty God, Lillie successfully raised her four boys into the educated and accomplished men they are today. Her home was not only a sanctuary for her children but also a refuge for their friends, many of whom still affectionately call her "Mom" to this day. Lillie's journey has been marked by overcoming a life filled with challenges, including dysfunction, church hurt, domestic violence, the loss of loved ones, and various health scares. Despite these trials, she has emerged as a dynamic, healed woman of God. Her story of resilience is beautifully captured in the "All Eyes On Us" chapter, where her strength and dedication to her family shine through.

God has blessed Lillie with many gifts and talents, including a profound ability to express herself through poetry. Her words resonate with the depth of her experiences and the strength of her faith. For over 12 years, she has been faithfully devoted to a dynamic end-time ministry that has captured her heart and soul.

After years of searching and self-discovery, Lillie has embraced her purpose and added "author" to her list of titles, sharing her testimony and journey with the world. Lillie Randle is a living testament to the power of faith, resilience, and unwavering love.

Poetry Reflections
By Lillie B. Randle

Dr. Sherley Lefevre, Ph.D.

Forgiveness

I don't want your love
When your love teaches hate
I don't want your joy
When your joy makes me unhappy
I don't need your care
When your care hurts me
I don't need your bread
When your bread leaves me hungry
You don't want my faith
When my faith keeps you
You don't want my word
When my word sustains you
You don't need my death
When my death resurrects you
You don't need my peace
When my peace frees you
What do I want?
What do I need?
What you want is what you need
And that's my forgiveness
For believing all the lies
You heard about me
You listened and believed the pain
From hurting people
What they neglected to tell
Was they had been forgiven
Yet they held onto the abuse
Got even angrier when I'd forgiven
Their abusers and users

That they prayed, begged
And sought mercy for
I love you and I hate the sin
So now that you know
Ask, Seek, Knock
And it will be given
Just simply believe the
Truth and not the lies
And I will give you
My forgiveness
After you've forgiven
Those who misled you
With Untruth
Always remember
I love you and I hate the sin!
At last, here's my forgiveness

Dr. Sherley Lefevre, Ph.D.

Dream, Imagine, Create

Dream on your pillow
Imagine in your brain
Create from your pain
Dream while sleep or awake
Imagine Beauty from the ashes
Create from an empty canvas
Dream BIG, Not small
Imagine you've answered His call
Create Art on the Mural
Dream very far
Imagine your car
Create an exquisite Star
Simply DREAM, IMAGINE, CREATE!

Hide Me Oh God...

In your Arms
In your loving Embrace
Where no harm
Will come nigh Thy Face
Under your Wings
With your faithfulness
As you watch out for Things
In my carelessness
In Your Tabernacle
In Your Word
Wherever You are
Hide me There
Let me dwell in Your Vine
So that I know I'm no longer mine
But FOREVER be Thine
Until You decide to-
End Time,
Hide Me Inside of You
So none of my enemies see me
But only the Truth
That you are my Victory
I simply want You to HIDE ME Oh GOD...

Dr. Sherley Lefevre, Ph.D.

A Simple Prayer

Merciful God
Oh kind and True
Thank you God
For loving me
Faithful Lord and King
Wonderful Master
Ruler of Everything
I praise You
From the bottom of my heart
I love you
Victory, You are!
Joy, You've given me
Oh, Abba,
Stay near me
Oh, Jesus keep me
Even when I've fallen apart
Gather me back together
Let a flashback start
To show the world that
You mend the brokenhearted
Hide me in your Word
Build my Faith by what I've heard
Teach me how to be guided by
Your Holy Spirit, especially while I cry
Let me understand how to live and die
In Jesus name AMEN!

Building Up

Walls are Building Up
Brick by Brick
Stainless steel Walls
Anger, misery and strife Calls
Destruction follows
Where now, you just feel hollow
Your demons of lust, hurt and pain creep In
Suicide joins the choir
Rehearsals start every morning
The Songs that burst from them, HATRED
Then Sin sick struck the right Chord
But wait you hear a sweet voice
That echoes from within
NOW every Wall, even the Stainless…
Hurry up and FALL; soundless
Yet, the tears DRIP
As the WALLS were being, Stripped!
And the HURT, PAIN WERE being Ripped
Now GENTLENESS and LOVE still GRIP
And start Building Up
NO thing is left
But Jesus' Blood
And His RIGHTEOUSNESS
That has a New Building up!

Dr. Sherley Lefevre, Ph.D.

All Eyes On Us

They must have thought we had curbside appeal
But those snooty stares would later reveal
'Dem was hungry after a hateful meal
Except it wasn't food they wanted to steal
Their side-eyed glances at…
Well, no one ever Rolled a Red carpet!
But, yes, you guessed it,
Their eyes sometimes hit the back of many heads
Instead, as if we had been pumped full of lead
And of course, the enemy yelling, "BETTER OFF DEAD!"
Children and adults alike
Acting like they were on strike
For their worthy cause
Of envy, hate just because
Jealousy was showing
With rejection growing
Up before our very eyes
It reminded me of my sons' styes
I thought we were to be in meditation
On the Word
Both day and night
But without hesitation
It was All Eyes On Us, in their line of sight
Prayer, Wednesday, Friday and Sunday Night
Maybe my understanding was lacking
Or was it because we were poverty stricken
That my former church started slacking
Soon it was time for my family to take our leave

The Runaway Bride

I'm sure no one even thought to grieve
Especially when, All Eyes On Us, looked relieved
Now, glad it wasn't curb appeal
That all was revealed
I think they do like Window shopping
Because they showed no signs of stopping
I do pray they are done with their game
They won't have anybody to blame
Especially, instead of All Eyes On Us,
God's eyes will be on them
When we see Jesus face to face
After running this Christian race
We have a promise in Isaiah 54:17
About no weapon prospering
And standing against them in judgment
Now, I get what He meant
About the least little ones?
This is why I choose Love and Victory
Over Hate and Mockery
Because I want my foes, friends and family
To hear 'Well done' in the end
No longer caring if All Eyes are On Us
But to keep Our Eyes
On The Amazing Prize

PART III
Scriptures & Prayers

Note to the Reader:

As you navigate the journey of healing from church hurt, know that you are not alone. The pain you've experienced is real, and so is the love and comfort that God offers to you. Prayer is a powerful tool that allows us to connect with God, express our deepest emotions, and invite His healing presence into our lives.

The following prayers have been crafted with your healing in mind. They are meant to be a source of comfort, strength, and renewal as you walk through this season of restoration. Whether you pray them as written or adapt them to your situation, I encourage you to bring your heart fully before God. Allow these words to guide you as you seek His peace, forgiveness, and wisdom.

Take your time with each prayer. Let the words sink in and be open to what God wants to say to you in these moments. Remember that healing is a process, and God is with you every step of the way. May these prayers be a balm for your soul and a light on your path as you move toward wholeness in Christ.

Prayer for Healing from Church Hurt

Dear Lord,

I come before You with a heart weighed down by pain and disappointment. The hurt I've experienced within the church has left deep scars, and I struggle to find peace. I ask for Your healing touch upon my heart, Lord. Help me to forgive those who have hurt me and release the bitterness that clings to my soul. Restore my trust in You and in the body of Christ. Show me how to love again, even when it feels difficult. In Your name, I pray. Amen.

Prayer for Restoration of Faith

Heavenly Father,

My faith has been shaken by the actions of others within the church, and I feel lost. I ask that You restore my faith, not in man, but in You. Remind me that You are perfect, even when people are not. Strengthen my resolve to follow You, despite the imperfections I see in others. Let my faith be grounded in Your Word and Your love, and not in the actions of those who have hurt me. Guide me back to the place where I can worship You with a whole heart. Amen.

Prayer for Forgiveness

Gracious God,

I confess that I've been holding onto anger and resentment towards those who have hurt me in the church. I know that harboring unforgiveness only harms my own soul. Today, I choose to forgive. I release the pain into Your hands and ask that You help me to truly forgive as You have forgiven me. Let my heart be free from the chains of bitterness and let love take its place. Heal the wounds that unforgiveness has caused and fill me with Your peace. Amen.

Prayer for Reconciliation

Lord Jesus,

You are the Prince of Peace and the Restorer of broken relationships. I pray for reconciliation within the church body. Where there has been division and strife, bring unity and understanding. Help us to see each other through Your eyes, with compassion and grace. Let us seek to heal rather than hurt, to build up rather than tear down. May Your love be the bond that brings us together, and may we reflect Your heart in our relationships with one another. Amen.

Prayer for Courage to Return

Dear God,

Fear and hurt have kept me away from the church for too long. I pray for the courage to return, not just to the physical building, but to the fellowship of believers. Give me the strength to overcome the memories of past hurts and to trust in Your plan for me. Lead me to a community where I can grow in my faith and serve You with joy. Let my return be a testimony of Your healing power and a step towards the restoration of my soul. Amen.

Prayer for Wisdom in Choosing a Church Home

Heavenly Father,

As I seek a new church home, I ask for Your wisdom and guidance. Help me to discern where You are leading me. Show me a place where I can find spiritual nourishment, genuine community, and a place to use my gifts for Your glory. Protect me from environments that would cause harm and guide me to a place where I can flourish in my faith. May Your Holy Spirit direct my steps and give me peace in my decision. Amen.

Scriptures for Healing and Restoration

Psalm 147:3 (NIV)

"He heals the brokenhearted and binds up their wounds."

When your heart is shattered by hurt, remember that God is near to heal and restore you. His love is the balm that mends the deepest wounds.

Isaiah 61:1 (NIV)

"The Spirit of the Sovereign Lord is on me, because the Lord has anointed me to proclaim good news to the poor. He has sent me to bind up the brokenhearted, to proclaim freedom for the captives and release from darkness for the prisoners."

This verse reminds us that Jesus came to bring healing and freedom. No matter how deep the hurt, His purpose is to restore and set you free from the pain that binds you.

Isaiah 61:1 (NIV)

"The Spirit of the Sovereign Lord is on me, because the Lord has anointed me to proclaim good news to the poor. He has sent me to bind up the brokenhearted, to proclaim freedom for the captives and release from darkness for the prisoners."

This verse reminds us that Jesus came to bring healing and freedom. No matter how deep the hurt, His purpose is to restore and set you free from the pain that binds you.

Matthew 11:28-30 (NIV)

"Come to me, all you who are weary and burdened, and I will give you rest. Take my yoke upon you and learn from me, for I am gentle and humble in heart, and you will find rest for your souls. For my yoke is easy and my burden is light."

When you feel overwhelmed by the weight of hurt, Jesus invites you to find rest in Him. His gentle care offers comfort and peace for your weary soul.

Romans 12:19 (NIV)

"Do not take revenge, my dear friends, but leave room for God's wrath, for it is written: 'It is mine to avenge; I will repay,' says the Lord."

Letting go of the desire for revenge and trusting God to bring justice allows you to focus on healing. He sees every wrong and promises to make things right in His perfect timing.

Ephesians 4:31-32 (NIV)

"Get rid of all bitterness, rage and anger, brawling and slander, along with every form of malice. Be kind and compassionate to one another, forgiving each other, just as in Christ God forgave you."

God calls us to release bitterness and embrace forgiveness. This scripture encourages you to let go of negative emotions and choose kindness and compassion, just as Christ has shown toward you.

2 Corinthians 1:3-4 (NIV)

"Praise be to the God and Father of our Lord Jesus Christ, the Father of compassion and the God of all comfort, who comforts us in all our troubles, so that we can comfort those in any trouble with the comfort we ourselves receive from God."

God's comfort is available to you in every situation. As you receive His comfort, you are also equipped to extend that same comfort to others who are hurting.

James 1:5 (NIV)

"If any of you lacks wisdom, you should ask God, who gives generously to all without finding fault, and it will be given to you."

In times of confusion or decision-making, especially when choosing a new church home or seeking guidance, God promises to provide wisdom generously to those who ask.

1 Peter 5:7 (NIV)

"Cast all your anxiety on him because he cares for you."

God invites you to bring all your worries, fears, and pain to Him. His love for you is deep and He cares about every detail of your life.

Hebrews 10:24-25 (NIV)

"And let us consider how we may spur one another on toward love and good deeds, not giving up meeting together, as some are in the habit of doing, but encouraging one another—and all the more as you see the Day approaching."

Though hurt may make you hesitant to engage with the church, this verse encourages you to seek out fellowship and community, where you can give and receive encouragement.

Psalm 34:18 (NIV)

"The Lord is close to the brokenhearted and saves those who are crushed in spirit."

God's presence is near when you are brokenhearted. He offers salvation and comfort when you feel crushed by the weight of your pain.

Scriptures on Effective Leadership

1 Peter 5:2-3 (NIV)

"Be shepherds of God's flock that is under your care, watching over them—not because you must, but because you are willing, as God wants you to be; not pursuing dishonest gain, but eager to serve; not lording it over those entrusted to you, but being examples to the flock."

True leaders in the church are called to shepherd God's people with a willing heart, serving eagerly and leading by example, rather than dominating or exploiting those they lead.

Matthew 20:25-28 (NIV)

"Jesus called them together and said, 'You know that the rulers of the Gentiles lord it over them, and their high officials exercise authority over them. Not so with you. Instead, whoever wants to become great among you must be your servant, and whoever wants to be first must be your slave—just as the Son of Man did not come to be served, but to serve, and to give his life as a ransom for many.'"

Effective leadership in the church is characterized by servanthood. Jesus teaches that greatness in His kingdom comes through humility and a willingness to serve others selflessly.

Titus 1:7-9 (NIV)

"Since an overseer manages God's household, he must be blameless—not overbearing, not quick-tempered, not given to drunkenness, not violent, not pursuing dishonest gain. Rather, he must be hospitable, one who loves what is good, who is self-controlled, upright, holy and disciplined. He must hold firmly to the trustworthy message as it has been taught, so that he can encourage others by sound doctrine and refute those who oppose it."

Effective church leaders are called to embody blamelessness, self-control, and sound doctrine. Their lives should reflect godly character, and they should be able to teach and encourage others while refuting falsehood.

James 3:1 (NIV)

"Not many of you should become teachers, my fellow believers, because you know that we who teach will be judged more strictly."

This verse reminds leaders of the gravity of their responsibility. Those who teach and lead in the church are held to a higher standard and must be diligent in their conduct and instruction.

1 Timothy 3:2-3 (NIV)

"Now the overseer is to be above reproach, faithful to his wife, temperate, self-controlled, respectable, hospitable, able to teach, not given to drunkenness, not violent but gentle, not quarrelsome, not a lover of money."

Leaders in the church are called to live lives that are above reproach, displaying self-control, gentleness, and hospitality. Their character should reflect the qualities that honor God and serve the community.

Philippians 2:3-4 (NIV)

"Do nothing out of selfish ambition or vain conceit. Rather, in humility value others above yourselves, not looking to your own interests but each of you to the interests of the others."

Effective leadership requires humility and a focus on the well-being of others. Leaders are to value others above themselves, serving with a selfless attitude.

1 Corinthians 4:2 (NIV)

"Now it is required that those who have been given a trust must prove faithful."

Faithfulness is essential for leaders entrusted with responsibility. Leaders must be reliable and steadfast in fulfilling the duties and responsibilities given to them by God.

Acts 20:28 (NIV)

"Keep watch over yourselves and all the flock of which the Holy Spirit has made you overseers. Be shepherds of the church of God, which he bought with his own blood."

Leaders are called to be vigilant both in their personal lives and in their care for the church. They must recognize the value of the people they lead, understanding that Christ purchased the Church with His own blood.

Proverbs 11:14 (NIV)

"For lack of guidance a nation falls, but victory is won through many advisers."

Effective leadership is strengthened by wise counsel. Leaders should seek guidance from others and value the input of trusted advisors to ensure success and avoid failure.

Made in the USA
Columbia, SC
06 October 2024